Napoleon's Maxims

for

Business Leaders

Napoleon's Maxims

for

Business Leaders

Guy Forsyth

A hardcover edition of this book was published in 2023 by Amazon

Napoleon's maxims for business leaders © 2020 by Guy V.J Forsyth

Translated by Amazon into languages on their site.

Second Edition published in 2023

ISBN 9781923007819

Table of Contents

About the Author

Guy Forsyth is an advisor and consultant to some of the worlds leading corporations. Specialising in the area's of leadership and management, business consulting and organisational change, he has worked with both the public and the private sectors. Graduating from the universities of NSW and Canberra with qualifications in Commerce, Law, and a doctorate in management, he has lectured in leadership and management, and conducted training in leadership and ethics at the Australian War College. He has been awarded the Prince of Wales Award for his services to the Royal Australian Navy. A keen student of military history, he has read widely on the various campaigns of many leaders with a primary interest in the Napoleonic period. He also has a deep interest in leadership development and leader personalities. Guy's work as a consultant provides advice in the areas of leadership, strategic management, performance, change management and ethics. He lives in Australia.

Acknowledgements

This book has developed over a period of time by successively adding layers of additional and specialised expertise. I have been greatly assisted by several people that have enabled the book to take on a character far greater than simply being a contemporary analysis of Napoleon's maxims.

The greatest contribution to this book has come from Katherine Hilyard, Managing Director of People and Strategy. Her insight and expertise in the area of leadership, management and human resources in general has been instrumental. The structure of this book is in no small part a result of her suggestions and broad exposure to leadership and management literature.

Several people have worked diligently to assist me in crafting the final version of this book into a form that is, hopefully, credible and readable. This has been achieved with the assistance of Margaret Carew-Reid, Carol Robinson and Kaaren Sutcliffe. Their significant involvement with political leadership and extensive background in document editing and writing have helped make this book far more relevant.

Timeline of Napoleon's life

1769	Born in Corsica
1779	Enters Brienne Military College
1784	Enters Ecole Royale Militaire, Paris
1785	Graduates as Second Lieutenant in Artillery
1793	Battle of Toulon
1795	Suppresses counter revolution in Paris
1796	Marries Rose de Beuharnais
1797	First Italian Campaign
	Plans invasion of England/invades Ireland
1798	Egyptian Campaign
1799	Elected First Consul of France
1800	Second Italian Campaign
1801	Closes Continental ports to Britain
1802	Promulgates Code Napoleon
1804	Crowns Emperor of France
	Resumes plans for invasion of England
1805	Ulm-Austerlitz Campaign
1806	Prussian Campaign
1808	Commences Peninsular War
1809	Danube Campaign
	Divorces Rose de Beuharnais
1810	Marries Marie-Louise Habsburg
1811	Napoleon II born
1812	Russian Campaign
1813	Leipzig Campaign
1814	Campaign to defend France
	Abdication & exile to Elba
1815	Restored as Emperor
	Waterloo Campaign
1816	Abdication & exile to St Helena
1821	Dies on St Helena

Preface

After the Battle of Waterloo the allied nations resolved that Napoleon should never be allowed to regain control of the French nation again. He had already escaped his banishment to Elba, and so after that fateful battle he was, in 1815, once again committed to captivity, this time on the Isle of St Helena. While in exile he dictated his memoirs to a group of followers that had accompanied him to his final home at Longwood. During the development of his memoirs a series of tenets on the art of warfare emerged. These were catalogued in various works that proposed them as 'maxims'- self-evident truths based upon the experience acquired throughout an epic lifetime of achievement. These maxims have subsequently become prized for their insight into the military art of the time and the mind of one of history's most astounding individuals.

Napoleon's military maxims each have a specific message, and these have become the topic of study for, predominantly, military historians and students of the martial arts. The question for the reader is how might these military maxims be relevant to the business environment? The answer being that regardless of the area of human endeavour there are common and linking threads. Military institutions place a high priority on ensuring leadership is identified and fostered. It is perhaps the only profession where leadership training is a core requirement, and for good reason. Warfare is the most intense environment in which mankind unfortunately engages and one of the most serious enterprises for any society. Few wars have resulted in the victor remaining unscathed.

> Military action is important to the nation – it is the ground of death and life, the path of survival and destruction, so it is imperative to examine it
>
> Tsun Tsu – *The Art of War*.

The degree of change and uncertainty in the warfare environment transcends any other undertaking. For this reason military leaders are trained to the highest order to be able to lead under extreme circumstances. Only the best succeed in the conditions in which they might be tested. While business undertakings are far less dramatic in their outcome they can involve the survival or destruction of any entity. The spoils of business can be as significant as those of warfare. For survival in business, as in warfare, leadership is paramount.

In business it is becoming increasingly important that leaders have the skills to deliver in the dynamic commercial environment. Yet, leadership is rarely taught in business-based academic courses, and there are limited opportunities for executives to pursue further study in this area. We all know that time is money. As a result it is better spent on making money than studying leadership principles. The practical consequence is that many of today's business leaders basically emerge through good career management. Unfortunately, the rate of change and the expectations upon organisations and their leaders is increasing each year.

'Business is war' is often stated in response to the incessant demands placed upon executives. There is scant time for professional development. The status quo may be fine for now but while effective management enables an organisation to stay in business, good leadership ensures that it flourishes.

Leaders need to constantly reassess their abilities. It is not enough to simply assume that the way that things are being done is the best. Increasingly, businesses are required to plan with a degree of insight that goes beyond mere competition. Strategies are becoming more complex. Modern business leaders need to have the skills to inure them to the daily demands and pressures of competition and conflict. The military environment, therefore, is probably one of the best sources to look to for an environment in a state of change and chaos that approximates the environment within which the modern executive operates – albeit without the bloodshed.

Drawing upon military concepts and techniques is not as foreign as we might think: these concepts pervade our business and social cultures. Our use of techniques commonly found in warfare develops very early on in life. As an example, we all remember when we first learnt to drive and would try to coax our parents to give us the car keys whenever possible. The direct approach of asking to take the car for a drive was often rejected. Most of us learned quite quickly that offering to run an errand or go and pick up something from the shop would often elicit the car keys. Without knowing the difference between the effects of a frontal versus a flanking manoeuvre we were already employing the principles. The same principles apply in the political arena where a more circuitous route is often used to achieve the desired outcome. Most of us are aware of how often politicians dupe the public with agendas that divert our attention from their real motivation.

Regardless of whether it is in the commercial, social, political or military environment, it is myopic to believe that the wisdom in one sphere of human endeavour is not relevant to others.

Business texts are full of examples of strategies used by successful organisations to avoid taking on competitors directly. Apple Computers, for example, have managed to keep an entirely different computer platform from becoming extinct in the highly competitive technology market by pursuing niche markets such as education and graphics design, and so avoiding direct competition. They have consistently been innovative and clever in their marketing, to the point where their user base is stridently loyal. Their approach has always sought to flank the market rather than frontally assault it, and as a result they have survived when many pundits have written them off. Any leader in a particular profession can learn from leaders in another; in fact we can learn from any source if we are open to the possibility to learn. Regardless of whether it is in the social, business, political or military arena, human behaviour is indelibly similar and comparable.

This book primarily focuses on leadership. It looks at the character of leadership and the action of leaders. Whether some of these elements constitute leadership or management is subject to debate. Almost all of the books on leadership and management differ on what are the core attributes of leaders and managers. The very source of the two words brings this distinction between leadership and management into focus. The word 'manager' is a derivative of the Latin word for 'hand' (*manus*) and subsequently the root of the French word 'ménagerer', which forms the basis of the English usage, literally meaning 'the person that takes control of the horses behind the field of battle'. The word 'leader' is derived from a Norse word 'löder' which was used to describe the person that read the lodestone (a crude compass) used to direct the Viking ships to their destination. The distinction has grown from there to give people the impression that leaders have this heroic, visionary role while manager have a more mundane, practical function.

Although leadership and management have fundamental differences managers can be leaders and, by corollary, leaders need to manage. Successful leaders still possess certain character traits to motivate people to do things that they otherwise would not do, and successful managers have superior competencies

> 'Management has to do with efficiency, with making things run properly. Leadership in contrast is concerned with identity – why we are here; what our business is; what our destination, goals and mission are.'
>
> Warren Bennis – *On Becoming a Leader*

to achieve complex tasks. Most writers on leadership acknowledge that leaders will generally propose a vision that others follow. This could be just as true of someone in a management role. In fact, many managers are exactly that: a guide for their staff. But there is still a distinction, and while you may be a manager with leadership attributes there are still fundamental differences between good leaders and good managers. In short, leaders are fundamentally change agents: they move people in a new direction. Management, on the other hand, brings people together to focus their attention on a certain task. They are process agents: they co-ordinate, structure and direct people in a direction that has been set by the leader.

> 'Leaders establish the vision for the future and set the strategy for getting there; they cause change. They motivate and inspire others to go in the right direction ... Management is a set of processes that keep a system ...running'.
>
> John Kotter "A force for change: how leadership differs from management"

This book has been divided into two basic sections: *Leadership character* and *Leadership action*. The first section of this book focuses on the characteristics of leadership simply because leadership (whether exercised by a 'leader', a 'manager' or anyone else) does have a particular character, and this character comes through forcefully in Napoleon's maxims. This is not to imply that character is a primary aspect of leadership. In fact the study of leadership has demonstrated the converse. However, it is still regarded as an integral component and one which cannot be dismissed. The second section of this book covers the implementation of leadership. It deals with the principle organisational issues that Napoleon had to deal with. The action of leadership has been categorised into strategic thinking, organisation and people - the three fundamental components that require leadership and management in any organisation.

Each chapter has been structured as follows:

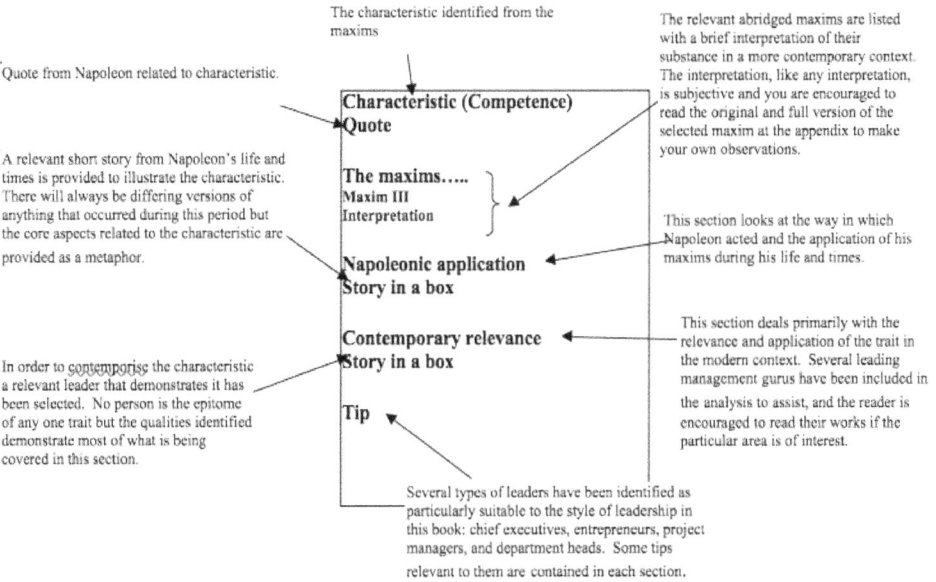

The characteristic identified from the maxims

The relevant abridged maxims are listed with a brief interpretation of their substance in a more contemporary context. The interpretation, like any interpretation, is subjective and you are encouraged to read the original and full version of the selected maxim at the appendix to make your own observations.

Quote from Napoleon related to characteristic.

Characteristic (Competence)
Quote

A relevant short story from Napoleon's life and times is provided to illustrate the characteristic. There will always be differing versions of anything that occurred during this period but the core aspects related to the characteristic are provided as a metaphor.

The maxims.....
Maxim III
Interpretation

Napoleonic application
Story in a box

This section looks at the way in which Napoleon acted and the application of his maxims during his life and times.

Contemporary relevance
Story in a box

This section deals primarily with the relevance and application of the trait in the modern context. Several leading management gurus have been included in the analysis to assist, and the reader is encouraged to read their works if the particular area is of interest.

In order to contemporise the characteristic a relevant leader that demonstrates it has been selected. No person is the epitome of any one trait but the qualities identified demonstrate most of what is being covered in this section.

Tip

Several types of leaders have been identified as particularly suitable to the style of leadership in this book: chief executives, entrepreneurs, project managers, and department heads. Some tips relevant to them are contained in each section.

At the end of the book is the appendix which contains the complete collection of Napoleon's military maxims from two sources: Lieutenant-General Sir George D'Aguilar's translation 'Napoleon's military maxims', published in 1831, and Professor Lucien E Henry's translation 'Napoleon's war maxims with his social and political thoughts', published in 1899. The former work contains 78 military maxims while the latter contains 115. Several authors have only drawn upon the D'Aguilar version partially because the originating work was divided into two books, the second book largely overlooked. In fact, Napoleon edited 531 maxims in total with most of them in the area of social and political thought. It has been the military ones, though, that have received the most attention. The process and development of them is well documented by the eminent historian and Napoleonic expert Professor D.G Chandler in 'The military maxims of Napoleon', written in 1987. Where appropriate the maxims used in the main text of the current work have been abridged in order to keep them as relevant as possible, but the reader is encouraged to consult the appendix for the complete maxims from the aforementioned versions.

'The core characteristics of effective leaders…include basic intelligence, clear and strong values, high levels of personal energy, the ability and desire to grow constantly, vision, infectious curiosity, a good memory and the ability to make followers feel good about themselves. [The] foundation characteristics… include empathy, predictability, persuasive capability, the ability to lead by personal example and communication skills. It is the weaving together, the dynamic interaction, of the characteristics on a day-by-day, minute-by-minute basis that allows truly effective leadership.'

Leaders of the Future – Peter Drucker

Even though leadership books abound with various qualities of leadership there is still no absolute definition. Fortunately the growing consensus among leadership experts and modern leaders is that 'effective leaders are made, not born' so the characteristics identified in this book will complement the body of knowledge on the character of leadership. Napoleon's maxims contain fundamental attributes of effective leadership. They provide an insight into one of the world's most charismatic and successful leaders.

Introduction

Napoleon's maxims are the direct result of the experience of being at the head of an army that conquered the largest area of Europe in history. They are also imbued with the personal characteristics of Napoleon himself. In order to understand the context and intent of the maxims we need to know something of the man. We may all know the caricatures of Napoleon in his trademark hat and overcoat with hand tucked into his waistcoat, but where did he come from and how did he rise to such prominence? Why was he followed, almost religiously, across Europe for over two decades?

Napoleon's start in life was fairly unremarkable for his time. Born as Napoleone Buonaparte on the small island of Corsica in the town of Ajaccio in 1769 he was one of five children. His parents claimed a noble lineage yet the reality was more akin to an upper middle class rural existence. Being of modest means they led an austere way of life. Napoleon's father held a position of influence in the town and used his associations to gain access to the Court of France, forever seeking to better his family's status. Napoleon's mother was strong willed, industrious and opportunistic. Her influence on Napoleon was far greater than any other person.

While growing up Napoleon was obsessed with the desire to become a soldier and would object violently when playing games at school if he was on the losing side. His older brother Joseph noted when he was only about nine: '…I had been placed by the teacher on the side under the Roman flag, Napoleone, impatient at finding himself under the Carthaginian flag, which was not that of the conqueror, would not rest until he had obtained permission for us to change places' Napoleon was also notorious for trading his school lunches with local soldiers to see how their rations tasted and hanging around barracks to hear their stories.

His siblings (of which there were six) would variously describe him as indomitable, pugnacious, stubborn and focussed. It certainly came as no surprise to those around him that he achieved the stellar heights that he did. His younger brother, Lucien, at 17, once ruefully stated with amazing prescience: '…he seems to me to be a tyrant, and I believe that he would be one, if he were king…'. Napoleon was not to take the throne of France for another twelve years yet those closest to him identified traits that would prove true enough.

As a soldier Napoleon encountered greater success in his profession than many before or after. However, he also suffered some of the greatest defeats in history. During the Napoleonic period campaigns were not a mere one day encounter where the winning side took the spoils. They could last weeks, or months. Movement of troops was mainly by foot with the artillery often man-handled across mountains and deserts or through mud and snow. The sheer determination to

1

succeed and the tenacity required were formidable qualities in Napoleon, his marshals and the soldiers. Many commentators have detailed the attributes which made the French army (*La Grande Armée*) of the time feared throughout Europe, but the one common factor that all are agreed upon is the character of its leaders.

As a commander Napoleon's achievements were nothing short of epic. Time and again Napoleon's army took on superior forces and defeated them in detail. Yet their position was not always ideal nor did they always have a technological or material advantage. Tactics, timing and ability often carried the day.

Visionary or warmonger? Liberator or dictator? Benefactor or egotist? Or perhaps all of these attributes. Admire or despise him the simple fact remains that he achieved more in his lifetime than many of us ever dream of—military conquest, social reform, exploration, political dominance, technological innovation, modernisation—change on a grand scale. Napoleon was not just a military dictator but a visionary, introducing reforms that have endured to this day, such as: a common law system, the Bank of France, reform of the court system, centralised government, national schooling, religious freedom, and so many more fundamentals that we take for granted.

In an era of revolution and one of the most tumultuous periods of history, Napoleon not only rose above the maelstrom, he flourished. What were the qualities that helped him to become so successful? How did he manage to be successful time and time again in several different spheres? What were the secrets of his success? Some of these secrets are encapsulated within his maxims. Just as *he* studied great leaders of history, so can we discover the attributes that he applied so successfully.

Leadership Character

A leader is a dealer in hope

N

Napoleon was a both a visionary and a change agent. Some have regarded him as the consummate leader. His abilities have been lauded for bringing together a country going through one of the greatest social upheavals in history and galvanising them into an indomitable fighting force. Possessing a superior intellect and unbridled energy, his generals and court attendants rarely questioned his judgement and certainly found it difficult to keep pace with his unrelenting pursuit of his 'star'. Even before his string of military successes he was once described by one of his Marshals as '... the sort of man of whom nature is sparing and who only appears on earth at intervals of centuries'.

When the French Revolution took place in 1789, Napoleon, aged 20, was a junior officer in the army. The Revolution had infused zealousness in the post revolutionary people of France. They had freed themselves from the oppression of tyranny and overthrown the monarchy that represented their subjugation. This fervour pervaded every section of society, and obviously the army as well. The leaders of the army were imbued with this newfound sense of purpose and were inspired by the constant success under Napoleon's leadership. As a result of the combination of charismatic leadership and the redefinition of warfare an unstoppable force emerged in the form of the *Grande Armée*.

Napoleon sought leaders with a diverse array of talents to lead the Grande Armée. Never one to let personality or appearance stand in the way of talent he chose people with the abilities needed to deliver his goals. The most outstanding were granted the title of Marshal, which often meant significant entitlements. He favoured courage and persistence in both his generals and soldiers but sought leaders that were also clever and lucky.[1] He held intellect in high regard, stating that a 'military leader must possess as much character as intellect' while remaining cautious of people that claimed the ability but lacked the credentials: 'There are scant resources to be found in men that have not had a primary education. They can feel keenly, they can sense, but they cannot analyse anything, and when they come up against novel circumstances they only perpetrate stupid mistakes'. He also believed that leaders should be able to take calculated risks in order to be successful.

---

[1] He would often ask his staff 'is he lucky?' before promoting someone to higher rank. He would also harangue his marshals to 'give me lucky generals'.

One of Napoleon's earliest protégés was a young Sergeant named Androche Junot. He first met Junot during his command of the artillery at the Battle of Toulon. Napoleon requested an aide to scribe communications for dispatch to the other field commanders. This role not only required someone who possessed good handwriting but composure under pressure in the face of battle. Despite being a non-combative role it was significant because the commander would issue orders to the rest of the army through these communications and it was vital that they were clearly and accurately transcribed and dispatched. Napoleon requested volunteers and Sergeant Junot was among them, and ultimately selected. During the battle, a canon ball fell close by Napoleon and Junot spraying young Junot's writing paper with sand. Unperturbed, he continued to take dictation and muttered 'Good, we won't need to blot this page'. Junot's humour and composure impressed Napoleon so much that he appointed him to his personal staff and commenced a long association with someone who was to become one of his finest marshals.

The quality of composure under pressure is but one of several attributes that Napoleon prized, with the others identified in the following maxim:

Maxim LXXIII

The first qualification in a General-in-chief is a cool head – that is, a head which receives just impressions, and estimates things and objects at their real value. He must not allow himself to be elated by good news, or depressed by bad. The impressions he receives, either successively or simultaneously in the course of the day, should be so classed as to take up only the exact place in his mind which they deserve to occupy; since it is upon a just comparison and consideration of the weight due to different impressions that the power of reasoning and of right judgement depends. Some men are so physically and morally constituted as to see everything through a highly coloured medium. They raise up a picture in the mind on every slight occasion, and give to every trivial occurrence a dramatic interest. But whatever knowledge, or talent, or courage, or other good qualities such men may possess, nature has not formed them for the command of armies, or the direction of great military operations.

In many ways this is a description of Napoleon's own equanimous persona – to remain cool and calm on the surface and yet be machine-like in the assimilation and prioritisation of information underneath. Remaining calm under pressure is a fundamental attribute of a good leader. The business environment is certainly not immune to stress and pressure. The more complex and dynamic the environment, the greater the need for a cool head and calming influence. Stress can lead to clouded judgement, poor decisions, speculative and subjective assessments. Calm and competent leadership restores the balance. Effective leaders assess each situation and apply sound reasoning. They also make others feel valued and engaged. This might mean active participation when your team is under pressure. It might mean becoming more involved with staff in a crisis situation by offering both verbal and physical support. For the same reason that a General appears before the army on the eve of a battle it important to be seen to be involved when times are tough. The worst leaders retreat from these situations and adopt an autocratic style while the more effective become involved yet remain calm, cool and collected.

Above all, the primary qualities that Napoleon prized in his leaders were courage, the ability to accept orders, and to act with total commitment. During his exile on St Helena he would recall in his memoirs those that had remained loyal and had distinguished themselves, while disparaging the venality of those that merely followed for personal gain.

Story in a box - Senior Command

Following the battle of Toulon in 1793 Napoleon was promoted to Brigadier General at 24 years of age. His success in that Battle brought him to Paris where he developed his political connections. In 1795 he succeeded in suppressing a post revolutionary uprising in Paris and was granted the command of the Army of the Interior: basically the protector of Paris. A short time later, drawing on his political associations, he secured the command of the Army of Italy.

Even though he had limited field experience the Directory charged him with removing the threat of Austrian incursions on French interests in Italy. The plan involved the army crossing the Alps and repelling the Austrians from northern Italy. At the age of only 26, Napoleon left Paris for the south of France to meet with his supporting generals.

The three generals over whom Napoleon had command were straight out of a young commander's worst nightmare. All three towered over him: Firstly there was General Serurier, 53, scarred face, aristocratic air, and known to have fought against the Corsicans when Napoleon was being born; second was General Augereau, 38, broad shouldered, hooked nose and chequered past, popular with his troops and highly sarcastic; and finally, General Massena, also 38, tall, dark and eagled eyed, stubborn and redoubtable.

Napoleon brought the plan for the conquest of Italy to them, and, in a mood of contemptuous indifference, began his relationship with them. While each General believed that they should have the command themselves, Napoleon managed to turn them around and even inspire support. At the end of the meeting General Augereau revealed to the other Generals that he found Napoleon somewhat frightening.

Ultimately Napoleon and his Generals pulled together an undisciplined brigade of rebels into a coherent fighting force and took control of Italy through a series of battles that made up what is regarded as Napoleon's finest campaign.

The transformation of the army was expressed succinctly by General Sir Archibald Wavell (later to become Field Marshall Lord Wavell as a result of his command of the English forces in the Middle East from 1940) in his book 'The Art of Generalship':

'If you can discover how a young unknown man inspired a ragged, mutinous, half-starved army and made it fight, how he gave it energy and momentum to march and fight as it did, how he dominated and controlled generals older and more experienced than himself, then you will have learnt something.'

No one has yet produced the definitive list of the qualities that are necessary for effective leadership mainly because different circumstances will dictate the most suitable qualities. One approach to leadership may be highly successful in one sphere but entirely inappropriate in another. This phenomenon was dealt with by Fred Fiedler in his book 'A theory of leadership effectiveness' which identified that certain leadership characteristics were more suitable to one environment than to another. Despite this, he proposed that certain common traits are applicable to any environment. This indicates that core traits are still relevant; however, the degree to which they are important will vary. Napoleon's maxims highlight several applicable characteristics that are as relevant in modern management and leadership as they were during his own era.

Competence

*What the mind of man can conceive and believe,
it can achieve.*

N

The maxims...

Maxim LXXVIII

*Read and re-read the Campaigns of Alexander, Hannibal, Caesar,
Gustavus Adolphus, Turenne, Eugene and Frederick; take them
for your model, that is the only way of becoming a great captain...*

Interpretation: Read the accounts of those that have gone before
you. Study them, understand them and apply them. Learn what
has made them a success.

Maxim LXXVII

*Generals-in-chief are guided by their own experience or genius.
Tactics, evolutions, the science of an artillery or engineering officer may be picked up from books, but the knowledge of the
great operations of war can only be acquired by experience, and
by the applied study of the campaigns of all the great captains...*

Interpretation: Knowledge of how to perform the duties of your
position can be acquired through study and training, but the
higher order skills that make you truly competent can only be
learnt through experience or by studying the experience
obtained by others.

Maxim LXXV

*It is the duty of the general of artillery to know of all the opera-
tions of the army, since he has to furnish arms and ammunition
to the different divisions composing it...*

Interpretation: You should be aware of the capabilities of the different parts of your organisation in order to be more effective in
your own part.

Maxim CXII

All the great captains have done their great deeds by conforming to the rules and natural principles of their art, and by the soundness of their plans, and the proportioned connection maintained between their means and the results they expect, between their efforts and the obstacle to be overcome. They have only succeeded by conforming to rules, whatever might have been the boldness of their designs and the extent of their success. It is on this ground alone that they are our models, and it is only by imitating them that we can hope to rival them.

Interpretation: All successful people operate according to fundamental principles that can be learnt and improved upon.

Napoleonic application

Napoleon was trained as an artillery officer yet demonstrated competence in military operations in general. He possessed a thorough understanding of the functioning and application of artillery through his training at the *École Royale Militaire* in Paris. His knowledge of military strategy and tactics was partially a result of his training and also self taught. He possessed a voracious desire to understand how others had achieved military success and applied himself assiduously to the attainment of the secrets of the military art. Building upon this knowledge Napoleon applied these techniques coupled with the technological advances and strategic doctrine of his time to achieve stellar success. While knowledge is essential, the practical application of knowledge is the other component of competence. The effective application of knowledge is necessary to achieve results. Appropriate application develops experience and is essential to build credibility and gain respect from those around you.

Story in a box - A soldier in the making

France had engaged in the conquest of Corsica while Napoleon was being born, and subsequently annexed it during his years as a young officer in the army. A spirit of resistance remained with the Corsicans, but was tempered by their overlords. Military force was a way of life. Despite their subjugation by a foreign power, it was still a common aspiration for boys in Corsica to want to become soldiers. The military, after all, was the most ostensible profession of the age and fundamental to the survival of nations. It also provided status, prestige and the opportunity for fame and fortune.

At school Napoleon took competitive games rather more seriously than his friends. His parents identified his pugnacious attitude early on and sent him to a military finishing school in Brienne, and from there he was ultimately selected for the *École Royale Militaire*. His aptitude in mathematics was his strong suit and ultimately a determining factor in his selection for training as an artillery officer. Somewhat fortuitously, the artillery was the army's elite corps and the only real avenue whereby officers of talent could gain promotion based on merit rather than title. Entry to the artillery corps required every student to undertake Bezout's *Cours de Mathematiques* for admission. This was an extensive and rigorous undertaking for any student. The course consisted of four volumes and was studied over a period of three years. Napoleon recognised the opportunity. He was good at mathematics and he was determined to succeed. The artillery corps was his vehicle to advancement and he knew it.

Although admission to the artillery corps required the completion of the three year course the option existed to take the exam on all four volumes at once. Success in this pursuit required a comprehensive awareness of the subject matter. In 1785 Napoleon decided that he would attempt the feat, taking the exam after only his first year. To make the achievement more credible he had to satisfy his examiner, the great French scientist Laplace. True to form, Napoleon managed to successfully pass a three year course in one. His commitment to study for this undertaking was an indication of his later attitude to pursue any goal with total dedication.

Napoleon's commitment to building competence continued beyond his years at the military academy. As a junior officer he was committed to self education and to a greater understanding of his craft. He read voraciously and would fill notebooks with copious collections of facts and details. His small quarters were filled with books of previous military campaigns, military doctrine and facts and figures about foreign powers. He was known to be able to describe in minute detail not only France's social, economic and geographic systems but those of most of Europe as well. He studied the great campaigns of Alexander, Julius Ceasar, Frederick, Hannibal and others. This was not done out of professional interest only, he wanted to know what they did to succeed and how to become like them. The tactics of their campaigns, their experiences and their attitudes all formed the person that was to replicate their feats with devastating effect.

Apart from the development of competence through the study of others Napoleon's maxims indicate that you should also know your opponent and your surrounding environment. It is all too easy to become cocooned in your position and not be aware of what is happening outside and across your organisation. The view from the top can become rarefied and unrealistic. Napoleon was not one to allow the status of his office prevent him from knowing what was going on at the lowest level of the army. His habit of going among the troops and the people was based upon a firm belief that the people at all levels of the organisation had something valuable to contribute. After all, he was not going to fight wars on his own. His participatory attitude was derived from a recognition of the multiplier effect of relying upon others: 'all men are created equal. It was always my custom to go amongst the soldiers and the rabble, to converse with them, hear their little histories and speak kindly to them. This I found the greatest benefit to me.' Being the monarch did not mean that he disregarded the opinion of those under him, often the reverse. Your own knowledge will always be augmented by those around you; the value of the people that are part of your team should never be underestimated.

Experience is a great teacher; unfortunately learning from experience is elusive to those of us in a hurry. This is where studying the experiences of others is so important. Through the understanding of other leader's techniques Napoleon formulated strategies and tactics that remained a constant part of his repertoire. Toward the end of his military career he said: 'I have fought over sixty battles and I have learned nothing which I did not know at the beginning'. His study of the great captains had prepared him well. Many prominent and successful business people will tell you the same thing: the fundamentals don't change, only the particulars.

Contemporary relevance

Competence is having the knowledge and expertise to discharge your responsibilities and be able to engender the trust of those you lead. It is fundamental in gaining respect from those around you. Clearly the advice to be drawn from the above maxims suggests that you should focus on a particular area of expertise, learn everything about it that is possible, look to the experience of others, and determine what successful leaders did to become successful.

In the business environment competence is not just confined to technical or intellectual capabilities. It also requires a comprehensive understanding of the environment in which your business operates. All too often we are too busy to look above the trench and survey the world around us. In any industry it is essential to understand as much as you can about both the organisation and the market in which it operates. This 'home work' can extend to examination and consultation with a vast range of people and publications, even beyond that which is typical for that industry. Thinking laterally about the sources of this information is also important. Information and knowledge should not be thought of simply as being confined to the shelves of bookshops or classrooms.

Story in a box - Warren Buffet

Singling out a modern business leader for competence is tough, and very subjective. But there is something that gives the second richest man in the US an edge – the fact that several million investors look to every move he makes.

While most of his friends were reading comic strips Buffett was reading the Wall Street Journal and analysing stocks and company performance figures. Buffet did not start out with the aim of owning a company or to be a multi-billionaire – in fact the term billionaire did not even exist – he just wanted never to struggle to make ends meet, and to do something that he enjoyed. He learnt very early on that simple trading transactions could result in making money: buy a carton of Coca Cola, split it up and, given the right conditions, people would pay a lot more for the cans of drink.

Buffet did not just study the market and the theories of investment, he lived it. He commenced his career with an investment firm that traded shares for their clients. This led to the acquisition of what was to become one of the most valuable stocks of all time in the company Berkshire Hathaway. If you had invested US$5 in Berkshire in 1965 you would now have a share worth over US$25,000; some of his original clients have recorded an increase in value of their investment of over 200,000 per cent! Considering that Buffet owns over 30% of Berkshire it is no wonder that his current net worth exceeds US$40 billion.

The secret of his success lay in the valuation of companies and possessing a keen nose for what is a good investment. He could smell an undervalued company and see how to transform it into a valuable one. Some might say there is a degree of good luck but Buffet examined every detail about every company and knew exactly what he was looking for. Combined with his extensive knowledge of how the stock market works and the need to maintain cash-flow and return high yields to his clients he approached every acquisition with clinical efficiency.

In a profession that is marked by historical analysis and performance evaluation, Buffet is aware of the importance of the here and now. He disdains buying stocks because they are rising, claiming it to be one of the worst reasons for doing so, and advises people that they should be more aware of the basics and what is happening today as a better indicator of how their investment will perform. Not one to simply rely upon the fundamental principles Buffet continuously refines his methods and stays one step ahead of the game. His techniques are hardly revolutionary. In a nutshell: learn everything that you can about the environment in which you are investing. A desire for knowledge and self improvement has been a continual process that has marked Buffet's career, and has certainly paid big dividends.

Remaining open

Competence is a core attribute of leadership because people need to know that you have the knowledge to be able to make credible decisions. You have the knowledge because you were open to learning it whether it was at a tertiary institution or on the job. The same principle applies in a position of leadership. Decision-making is not always conveniently assisted by having all the facts and figures at your fingertips. You often have to rely upon others to develop your own knowledge and experience rather than expect that others see you as having all the answers. In Dr Stephen R Covey's book 'Principle Centred Leadership', he advocates that competence is developed through an acceptance of continuous learning, whether through training or experience. The key is to remain open and willing to learn. Many of the world's most successful people have remained open simply because they were out of their depth on more than one occasion. This allowed them to seek other's advice and guidance and to learn from those around them. It did not mean that they were indecisive, more that they were willing to supplement their knowledge and experience with that of others. Leadership sometimes means accepting that you may not always have all the answers. The apparent contradiction is that you need the knowledge and experience to lead yet also need to be open and willing to learn to grow and improve. Balancing these is the key.

Applying knowledge

Acquiring knowledge is but one component of the competence equation – knowledge application is the other. Competence gained through experience and the application of the knowledge acquired is a fundamental recipe for successful leadership. You need to be able to demonstrate that you can deliver results. It is not enough to have the university medal in the subject, you must be able to practically apply the knowledge. This is where your experience and learning from other's experience is crucial. Studying the management and leadership techniques of people in your field, for example, is a fundamental requirement for the application of leadership principles obtained through theoretical learning, drawing on *their* experience to augment your own.

Technical knowledge and expertise are important at middle and lower levels in an organisation. As we move up the hierarchy greater breadth is required. Unfortunately, trading on technical expertise will eventually make you one-dimensional. This is fine if you want to be an expert in your field and happy to work in a narrow arena. However, specialisation is rarely the path to effective organisational leadership. MBA graduates do not just study accounting, finance and economics, they develop knowledge and awareness of a range of issues associated with the management and control of an organisation. While specialisation might see you to middle ranks you might not progress or succeed in higher positions if your focus is too specific. Experience and competence gained from seeing what happens in a variety of situations is invaluable. A well rounded knowledgeable leader has a multi-facetted background.

Summary

Knowledge and experience are the fundamentals of competence. Remaining open to learning and developing your expertise is essential but the character of leadership means being able to apply these things at the right time and in the right way. Competence enhances your credibility and is something that people will always identify as essential in leaders in the business environment. It is not simply found in text books and quite often is tested in the face of difficult situations. For this reason alone you should never underestimate the necessity to keep learning – from any source.

Leadership tips

Executives:

Bibliographies of business leaders are essential reading. The MBA only gave you part of the picture.

Project managers:

Obtain the "lessons learned" from other projects. Learn from other project managers experiences.

Entrepreneurs:

Fellow entrepreneurs love to tell the secrets of their success. The book stores are full of them, but don't forget the industry and peak bodies.

Responsibility

I have only one counsel for you – be master
N

The maxims...

Maxim LXVII

In war, the leader alone understands the importance of certain things, and he alone, of his own will and superior wisdom, conquers and overcomes all difficulties.

Interpretation: It is the responsibility of anyone in a leadership role to make decisions and pursue the desired course of action. Your abilities and resolve will be instrumental in overcoming difficulties.

Maxim LXXIII

... every General is culpable who undertakes the execution of a plan which he considers faulty. It is his duty to represent his reasons, to insist upon a change of plan; in short to give in his resignation rather than to allow himself to become the instrument of his army's ruin. Every General-in-chief who fights a battle in consequence of superior orders, with the certainty of losing it, is equally blameable. In this last-mentioned case, the General ought to refuse obedience; because blind obedience is due only to a military command given by a superior present on the spot at the moment of action. Being in possession of the real state of things, the superior has it then in his power to afford the necessary explanations to the person who executes his order...

Interpretation: If you are given responsibility for something then accept it and do whatever is necessary to succeed, or reject it and move on.

Maxim LXV

The same consequences which have uniformly attended long discussions and councils of war will follow at all times. They will terminate in the adoption of the worst course, which in war is always the most timid, or, if you will, the most prudent...

Interpretation: At the end of the day a committee can only act according to its mandate – it is a leader's responsibility to make decisions and act.

Nothing is more important in war than unity in the command; thus when there is war against but one power there should be but one army, acting on one line, and by one chief.

Interpretation: One person and only one person should be accountable in any organisational structure. The lines of responsibility should be clear to all that are involved.

Napoleonic application

Napoleon knew that in order to achieve his goals he had to take risks. Responsibility does not come without risk. From his earliest appointments Napoleon demonstrated a willingness to take on responsibility and control. He knew that great accomplishments commenced with small successes. Inherently ambitious and with a drive to succeed he placed himself in situations that would test him so as to prove his ability to those around him. As a junior officer he wrote in one of his notebooks 'I must succeed at everything I do'. This attitude typified his approach to both military and political involvement.

Story in a box – The Battle of Toulon (1793)

Following the French Revolution in 1789 the country was divided between the Jacobins and the Royalists. The Royalists were primarily supported by England in an effort to restore the 'natural order' of things and reinstate the Bourbon monarchy. The south of France was still stridently loyal to the monarchy and, to that end, invited the English to support their cause. One of the areas where the English had a foot-hold on mainland France was the port town of Toulon. This was France's main naval base in the Mediterranean yet English and Spanish ships were in its harbour. It also presented a real risk to the rest of Republican France from invasion. An even greater affront was that the ships in the port were no less than Admiral Hood's Fleet under the Command of Sir Sidney Smith, one of Lord Admiral Nelson's best commanders and destroyers of French vessels.

The French army was instructed by the Directory to take the town of Toulon and evict the fleet. In order to do so there would need to be heavy reliance upon artillery, and so an able artillery officer was required urgently. Captain Bonaparte was identified as a suitable candidate and was summonsed to attend for duty at army headquarters just outside Toulon. Although reluctant at first to leave Corsica, Napoleon threw himself into his new assignment with vigour. He didn't have much to work with in his first significant posting and the command structure was infected with the same nepotism and incompetence that pervaded all of the *ancient regime* armies. The quality of the troops and materiel was not far behind with untrained men that had never seen active service and a potpourri of various artillery pieces. Nonetheless, he and his fellow officers were given a clear directive: take the fort at Toulon and evict the English from the harbour. Not a simple affair, even with trained men and sufficient equipment.

The commander of the French force, General Carteaux, was courageous and decisive yet utterly incompetent. His bold plan of attack was to rain down fire from Captain Bonaparte's artillery on the town and the English fleet and then storm the fort with the same ardour that had seen him and his comrades take the Bastille on that glorious day in 1789. Napoleon, on the other hand, saw that that the key lay in the geographic advantage that the French had, and not in risking a direct confrontation with limited and poor resources. His observation of the landscape was such as to determine the vulnerability of the English ships, being the key to the forts supply and protection. The bay where the ships were anchored was controlled by two narrow passes lined by hills that overlooked both the bay and the fort. If the peninsular hills could be taken then the English Fleet would be trapped and easily destroyed by the artillery. If the Fleet was destroyed then the Fort would have no support and would capitulate. Despite the logic of Napoleon's plan his superior officer rejected it and pressed for an all out assault. As expected, the initial attempt failed and only resulted in casualties on both sides. Preparations were made for another assault at the next opportunity.

Napoleon again presented his plan and once more it was rejected by his superior commander. Undeterred, Napoleon began to agitate among his contacts in Paris to show why the present strategy was flawed and would never see the fort fall. He prepared an extensive plan and detailed what he had done and would do to ensure that *his* plan succeeded. The report was peppered with references to the action he had taken to ensure the success of the operation: "I have taken measures…", "I have established…", "I have required…". Clearly he was taking complete responsibility for the success or failure of the proposal and pinning his hopes for recognition on it. While the tactics and preparations were listed in detail he also set about building up his armaments and ensuring that his troops were trained and ready for the task ahead. He believed in the plan and was prepared to stand by it. In the meantime, the commanding officer for the campaign had been replaced (in no small part due to Napoleon's incessant complaints of incompetence) by someone that fully supported his plan – he now had free rein to proceed.

The English had fortified their position and made their position impregnable with significant enhancements to the defence of the peninsula – exactly where Napoleon had previously advised he would secure victory – having realised the precariousness of their position in line with Napoleon's observations. Despite this minor set-back, and already fully committed to the plan, the newly appointed commander and also newly promoted Major Bonaparte led the assault. Following fierce resistance the fortifications on the peninsular fell and the English fleet immediately set sail to avoid the risk of being hemmed in. His plan had worked. Without the fleet the fort at Toulon quickly capitulated and the job was done.

Napoleon's commander offered effusive praise for the tenacity and dedication shown by the young Bonaparte: 'I lack words to convey Bonaparte's merit to you; much knowledge, equal intelligence and too much bravery; that is but a feeble sketch of this rare officer's virtues…' Napoleon received full credit for the campaign and was subsequently promoted Brigadier-General at the age of 24.

No undertaking was too grand, and no obstacle was too great to overcome. Napoleon would often approach a difficult task with unbridled enthusiasm and positive energy that inspired those around him. A problem was seen as a challenge, an obstacle as an opportunity. *Carpe diem* could have been his catch-cry for in one of his comments on the art of war he said 'In war as in policy, the lost moment never returns'. As a result he stepped up to the mark on any occasion and confronted the situation with a belief that it would be a success.

Napoleon was also big on governance. He ensured that he had coverage for all the operations that he undertook and that this remained in place to support his often lengthy campaigns. He made sure that the people in high places knew the consequences of their action or inaction. He ensured that all steps had been taken to bring success and that the correct lines of accountability were in place. Whether the responsibility was to supply his army or to manage the government finances people were assigned and relied upon to deliver – and they knew it.

Contemporary relevance

Responsibility requires courage and integrity. Courage to stand alone and be counted. Integrity to do what you believe in. Leadership requires us to make decisions – and decision-making involves personal risk. It also requires determination and resolution. A leader is ultimately responsible for the things assigned to them which impose accountability to external parties such as shareholders, customers and society in general.

It is a fact of life that over the course of your career you will have an increased amount of responsibility placed upon you. This responsibility cannot be abrogated because of external factors beyond your control; these are the very things that we are expected to deal with. It will often be the 'unseen' things that present you with the greatest challenges and which differentiates the successful from the mediocre. A lack of foresight is not an appropriate excuse for relinquishing responsibility for the occurrence of an unforeseen event. This is one of the paradoxes of leadership. If you accept the role then you also accept the responsibility for events that might not be within your control.

Story in a box – President Harry S. Truman

On the evening of April 12, 1945 the President of the United States of America, Franklin D Roosevelt, died in office. The world was in the midst of the greatest calamity in human history, and America was caught right in the middle. With a war raging in Europe against Nazi Germany and in the Pacific against Imperial Japan, Vice President Truman faced one of the greatest baptisms by fire of any leader in history.

The death of Roosevelt sent shock waves through the allied powers. What would the new President be like? Would he have the ability to see the war in the Pacific to a conclusion? How would he deal with the pacification of Europe? These questions hung heavily in the air largely because Truman had held the Office of Vice President for just 82 days prior to Roosevelt's death and had little, if any, recent contact with the former President or with the foreign powers. Apprehensions existed as to whether Truman had the knowledge and ability considering that Roosevelt had been in office for over twelve years and governed in an environment of wartime secrecy. But the farm boy from Independence Missouri was made of stronger stuff than anyone had realised.

It was understandable that the people in the Oval office admired and respected the former President and knew that he would to be a tough act to follow. Rather than adopt the obvious solution of replacing the existing staff with his own confidants Truman instead deferred to their expertise, wanting to be seen as acknowledging their importance. This took a strong character to be prepared to at once be held accountable for decisions and at the same time to trust and respect those around him to provide the correct advice and guidance. It was a difficult balancing act in the early stages of Truman's presidency to walk the line between avoiding the appearance of being a puppet president and yet possessing the ability to establish his imprimatur on a role that the previous incumbent dominated. Nonetheless, he devolved responsibility and encouraged his staff to be forthright and open. He engendered trust and developed a loyal support base from people that previously had little or no involvement with him

Truman recognised immediately that any decision made for the country was ultimately his responsibility. His Presidency was characterised by the acceptance of responsibility – his desk in the Oval office bore the plaque with the simple words: 'The buck stops here'.

This demonstrated to those around him that he saw himself as being accountable and therefore that he was the one in charge – not the administration. If there was an important decision to be made, then he would make it.

During his term Truman faced daunting challenges in a period of tumultuous change. Equal to the task, he summed up his capacity to take on these responsibilities with the immortal quip: 'If you can't take the heat, then get out of the kitchen'. Presiding over the end of World War II and the embarkation of the US in the Cold War, Truman made numerous monumental and controversial decisions, such as calling for the unconditional surrender of both Nazi Germany and Japan, sacking General Douglas MacArthur in the Korean War, and defying Stalin and Communist

Russia incursions in Europe and Asia. But perhaps the most vexing decision that has faced any leader in any sphere was the one made on 25 July 1945 – to drop a nuclear bomb on Japan. Bearing the knowledge and responsibility for this in silence Truman made a decision that has remained controversial to this day.

Truman knew that any decision rested squarely with him because he ultimately appointed the people that advised him and who carried out government policy. If the policies delivered then he would be praised, but if they did not then he would have to accept the criticism and censure of the public. In his address to the nation ending his term of Presidency, Truman echoed the attitude that he brought to the office with these words: 'The President, whoever he is, has to decide. He can't pass the buck to anybody. No one else can do the deciding for him. That's his job.'

Truman has gone down in history with the recognition of being as close to a 'near perfect' President as possible, but his importance was immortalised by the words of Winston Churchill, when he recalled their first meeting in Potsdam in 1945:

'I must confess, sir, I held you in very low regard then. I loathed your taking the place of Franklin Roosevelt...I misjudged you badly. Since that time, you more than any other man, have saved Western civilisation.'

Regardless of what action he took, Truman stepped up to the plate and took on the responsibility of a role in a period of dramatic change with an attitude that demonstrated the courage and commitment required of effective leadership responsibility.

Know yourself

In order to accept greater responsibility you must first 'know yourself'. In Warren Bennis' book 'On becoming a leader' he talks of four stages that any person must go through to know themselves. His second step is to 'accept responsibility – blame no one'. In Bennis' view this should be intuitively obvious to every leader but all too often we see leaders playing the 'blame game'. They externalise the concept of responsibility. Everyone else is somehow at fault for their failures. Leadership requires that we understand that we must accept responsibility for our failures. As a leader what you do to succeed or fail is entirely dependent upon how you lead others. It is important to 'know thyself'[2], that is, understand your style and your motivations before making any decision on the information before you. In an article by Colin Benjamin titled 'Enduring Wisdom' he states that 'unless there is equal time given to the gathering of human intelligence and intelligent interpretation – understanding the cultural differences between your manage-ment and leadership styles and those of your communication channels – there is every chance of failure.'

---

[2] It is interesting to note that the words 'know thyself' were inscribed above the entrance of the Temple of the Oracle at Delphi. Throughout the early period of Greek history many consulted the Oracle at Delphi for advice. Alexander the Great being a notable visitor. The advice was often cryptic leaving the interpretation to the recipient. The predisposition and nature of the recipient was a decisive factor in how the advice was implemented.

In Winston Churchill's words 'the price of greatness is responsibility'. Some of us decide to avoid promotion at a certain point in our career because we do not believe that the remuneration, stress or effort is worth the responsibility that goes with it. Others pursue greater responsibility despite these consequences. Then there are those who are not given the opportunity to accept more responsibility but desire it, which can often be a difficult fact to face. If this is the case then it is important to ask yourself why. Why do others see you as not possessing the attributes to accept greater responsibility? Could it be that they perceive that your words do not match your actions, or visa versa? Could it be that your ambition has outstripped your capacity or authority? Every leader needs to ensure that their rhetoric stacks up against their beliefs. Our core belief system is fundamental to how we act. You cannot hope to succeed in leading people without words matching your actions.

Act ethically

Acting ethically is central to responsibility because the enforcement of responsibility is based upon a belief in what constitutes acceptable or appropriate behaviour. In any collective, be it country, corporation or club, the interaction between people imposes a responsibility on all to behave according to certain rules. Any rule or law in society is fundamentally based upon ethical considerations of what is equitable for the whole. A leader is charged with the responsibility to uphold ethical principles through their actions by rewarding what is 'right' and to disincentive what is 'wrong'. To accept this responsibility it is necessary to also have the moral integrity to enforce the things that the society or organisation dictates. Every person in a position of leadership has to ask themselves whether they believe in the principles and standards they are asked to uphold.

Responsibility transcends personal needs and aspirations. It imposes obligations on us towards the people, and organisations that we lead. As a result it is becoming increasingly more important for organisations to behave properly in a social context as well. The obligation of executives to run corporations that have a social conscience is now, more than ever, a fundamental consideration. Organisations have been forced by society to be more environmentally sensitive, more ethical, and more accountable. We have seen the move from the 'bottom line' being just about profit to the 'quadruple bottom line' which now imposes social, legal, environmental, and most recently, ethical responsibilities upon organisations. Leaders of these organisations are being forced by their society to be more accountable and to adopt these principles because organisations are intrinsic parts of our society whether we, and they, like it or not. Corporate leaders need to act in a socially responsible manner if the organisations they lead are to endure and be respected by the general public. Respect and integrity starts on the inside.

Self-discipline

Accepting responsibility also requires self-discipline. Leadership requires effort on a number of fronts and these are sometimes not easy to accomplish unless self-discipline is exercised. We accept responsibility because we are prepared to be held accountable for our actions and, more importantly, the actions of others. We can only make this sort of commitment when we believe in both ourselves and those around us. This attitude engenders respect among those that we lead. We are seen to 'walk the talk'. Our actions and words are inspiring because we believe in them. Leaders are able to lead because people identify attributes in them that they respect and admire. Decision-making is difficult, delivering to expectations takes conviction. You need to have the motivation and persistence to keep going. Accepting the responsibility to succeed and lead others requires self-discipline to keep going despite the obstacles, controversies and set-backs.

Governance

One of the key responsibilities of leadership is to ensure that adequate governance is in place. Decision-makers must be identified before decisions can be ratified. Governance structures are about allocating decision-making responsibility. If the appropriate structures are not in place to support sound decision-making then your first action should be to see that you and others have the necessary responsibility for the position you hold and the decisions you are charged to make. If the organisation does not have the systems in place then it is the leader's responsibility to ensure that it does. Without suitable governance arrangements you are exposed to being held responsible for every decision.

The situation might go something like this: you are given responsibility to deliver a new product or service for the organisation; there is a need to move fast so you crash all the necessary steps together in order to deliver; then things start to go wrong; you need more money, you need to make changes to the original solution, you need to obtain corporate approval to engage external resources – but there is no-one willing to do so; the project falls in a heap, or worse, and you are held responsible for the fallout.

The establishment of a governance structure is vital to the success of any initiative. It is necessary to be aware of what constitutes good practice in governance. This will make you far more persuasive in establishing the correct structure that is appropriate for your organisation or undertaking. Every leader should understand the principles of good governance and insist that they are followed. If you establish a governance structure and make people aware of their obligations yet things still don't change, then chances are you might just be in the wrong organisation!

Anyone that is given the responsibility to deliver something for their organisation should ensure that they have the necessary authority to act. If you are directed to implement something without this then despite what you may think or what you are told, you will either have a very tough time in delivering or you will fail. To minimise the risk of failure there should be a process in place for approvals and changes. This should be clear to everyone in the governance structure to ensure the responsibility for approving changes to the original scope is accepted by all parties affected by the outcome.

Summary

Leadership means stepping up to the mark and being prepared to take risks for what you believe in or what you want to achieve; it imposes the responsibility for delivering results. It also imposes the obligation to be held accountable for your actions and the actions of others. Responsibility takes courage to accept the consequences of your actions. The responsibility imposed upon leaders is driven by the need to meet the expectations of those they serve, to behave equitably and in a socially acceptable manner. In order to meet this obligation, responsibility and accountability are delivered in an organisation through good governance. The implementing and oversight of good governance is primarily a leadership responsibility.

Leadership also imposes upon you an obligation to do what you are directed to do and to do it to the best of your ability. An organisation's values and behaviour should be an extension of its leader's values and behaviours. The effect of any organisation on society is a direct consequence of the actions of its leaders. If the moral integrity exists in the leaders of an organisation then this will emanate from the organisation and responsibility will be accepted as a natural consequence of the position of leadership. Only when this happens will your behaviour match your words. After all, an organisation's actions are ultimately a function of the conscience and integrity of its leaders.

Leadership tips

Executives:
Don't become another statistic of corporate failure – establish who is responsible and accountable at all levels of an organisation.

Project managers:
Effective governance arrangements will assist you in delivering the project and ensure the right levels of support are available to resolve issues and approve changes.

Entrepreneurs:
Accepting the role of production manager, marketing manager, designer, salesman, accountant, or corporate lawyer requires significant expertise and imposes significant risk. If you don't have the skills then buy them.

Intuition

In war there is but one favourable moment;
the great art is to seize it.

$\mathcal{N}$

The maxims...

Maxim XIX

The transition from the defensive to the offensive is one of the most delicate operations in war.

Interpretation: Moving from one state to another requires awareness of all the surrounding factors. Timing, tactics and opportunity are of fundamental importance in this operation.

Maxim LXX

The conduct of a general in a conquered country is full of difficulties. If severe, he irritates and increases the number of his enemies. If lenient, he gives birth to expectations which only render the abuses and vexations inseparable from war the more tolerable. A victorious General must know how to employ severity, justice, and mildness by turn, if he would allay sedition, or prevent it.

Interpretation: Always be aware of the environment in which you operate and tap into its undercurrents. Greater effect can be obtained through the careful exercise of discretion than to invoke the power of your position.

Maxim CXV

...It is by the eyes of the mind, the conjoint use of his reasoning powers that he sees, knows and judges. It is the faculty of seizing at once the connections which the ground bears to the nature of countries, it is a gift termed 'the soldiers eye', which great generals have received from nature...

Interpretation: Take as much detail in as possible and see the 'big picture'. Draw upon your inner knowledge and experience to look into the heart of a situation and come to a conclusion.

Napoleonic application

Napoleon had a feel for warfare that seemed innate. His ability to read the situation and act accordingly was often regarded as central to his genius. On the battlefield his timing was executed to perfection. He seemed to 'know' the right time and the right place to act; he realised that there is a precise moment upon which an outcome is decided – 'there is a moment in engagements when the least manoeuvre is decisive and gives victory; it is the one drop of water that makes the vessel run over' as he would sometimes say to his marshals. Seizing that precise moment and acting often led to a successful outcome. This intuition was not just about having the competence and knowledge in military affairs, but being in tune with the surrounding circumstances, being able to spot opportunities as they arise and taking advantage of them.

Story in a box – Napoleon seizes political control

Before Napoleon became the self-proclaimed Emperor of France he was able to take control of the country through a series of well executed political manoeuvres. His desire to become the country's supreme ruler after the revolutionary purge of the aristocracy could have been regarded as suicidal at the time. Aristocrats were beheaded mercilessly throughout the Terror and the memory of the abhorrence for the aristocracy was still palpable. In this climate it was unwise to be noticed with any royalist inclinations, let alone aspire to absolute power. Yet Napoleon did so and also resurrected all the trappings of the old regime! Such a situation did not come about without significant personal risk, and a singular ability to read the situation around him.

Other opportunities had arisen for Napoleon to come to power, yet he had rejected them. Absolute power was not his aim initially, however it became apparent that the capability of the governing body of France, known as the Directory, could certainly be improved upon. Timing and political nous were to prove critical to his success.

Napoleon had tasted power and administrative control after the Italian Campaign. He had effectively reorganised the entire Italian political landscape following French occupation; establishing several Republics and annexing large areas of Italy and her coastal islands. It was through this that he was able to gain an intimate understanding of the machinery of government. His return to France after the Italian campaign was perceived as a threat by the Directory. Napoleon played down the possibility of a military dictatorship by aligning himself with the intelligentsia rather than the Jacobins or any other politically charged group. Although he was acutely aware that he was in a position to mount a *coup*, he waited.

The Directory was also aware of the possibility of a putsch by Napoleon and the army, so attempted to marginalise his ever increasing political appeal. They commissioned him with the invasion of England knowing that such an undertaking was a make or break affair. The Royal Navy would be difficult, albeit almost impossible, to overcome so Napoleon postured towards an invasion and prevaricated to buy time. Foreseeing that the Directory would ultimately wear out their welcome with the people of France, he chose instead to mount a campaign in the Middle East under the auspices of a scientific venture to Egypt. This fascinated the population, and during his absence his reputation grew while the Directory effectively lost control.

The complexity of the French political landscape in 1799 was daunting to even a seasoned intriguer. Inflation had crippled the economy and the depredations of the army and the Directory had thrown them both into disrepute with the public. The memory of the Terror was still haunting, despite being ten years on from the Revolution, so any royalist revival was unlikely. When Napoleon returned from Egypt he was identified as a potential candidate for a new order. The conspirators and plotters for a new regime immediately solicited his support. Outwardly Napoleon coyly chose to identify with the Scientific institute which had accompanied the army to Egypt, and at the same time expressing support for the Directory all the while planning his coup.

The time was right to seize power – and he knew it. The skill with which Napoleon managed the highly political gamesmanship was outstanding. His intuition told him to remain non-partisan and to be seen as being without agenda; if anything to project an image of victim of the Directory's derision. Propaganda was used superbly to embellish his accomplishments and enhance his integrity. Above all, he was able to determine where the power lay and how to align himself with the right people, while simultaneously distancing himself from others. The end result was the election of a new government of which Napoleon was first consul. The application of intuition, his timing and political nous ended in triumph and paved the way for him to become supreme ruler of France.

Napoleon's maxim describe having a 'soldier's eye' in relation to decision-making. The French refer to this as *coup d'oeil,* meaning 'the power of the glance'; the ability to see things as they are in totality. Napoleon seemed to be able to construct a mind view of an area of military operation and know where the weak point would be in the enemy's position and where to locate his troops to exploit that weakness. During a battle he would have his forces conduct an operation at a specific time or place to achieve a decisive breakthrough. On many occasions his adversary could not see the point of a particular manoeuvre – until it was too late.

Contemporary relevance

The business environment is dynamic; posing complex problems and difficulties, often moving at a pace that does not allow the luxury of lengthy and extensive deliberation. In this context the use of intuition in decision-making becomes a real and necessary option. Applying the full suite of analytical tools to every decision in an unpredictable and fluid environment may result in missed opportunities and poor decisions. Time marches on, and unless we act events ultimately overtake us.

Story in a box – Richard Branson

Some people have a nose for business that just seems innate. Branson started his career selling things on the side at school. Nothing special; small items that others wanted, but he made a profit. While still at school he and a few friends saw the opportunity to start up a student magazine. To make money and expand the content of the paper they sold advertising space. The magazine became a successful little enterprise and Branson approached several celebrities for interviews to increase its reader appeal. To increase the magazines exposure further, he proposed the idea of selling music records through the magazine via mail order. After all, it was the swinging sixties and the music industry was exploding.

He and his colleagues were 'virgins in business' so the mail order label became Virgin Mail Order. It took off. Orders poured in. With business buoyant from the mail order business Branson proposed opening a store to sell to the general public. The first record store started modestly in the unused area of a shoe store but was set up to be a 'cool' place to go. Other stores followed with the same image of being a place for music enthusiasts to indulge their passion. The fledgling Virgin Records chain quickly spread across the UK. Every store worked to a common goal of doing what the customer wanted and making sure that they stayed in tune with customer needs.

Unsatisfied with just selling records, Branson decided that his record distribution business might be a good vehicle for up and coming artists to take their talents to market. Numerous recording artists were signed up with some of them ending up with hit albums, making Branson quite wealthy in his twenties. The idea of diversification then became the mantra of Branson and Virgin began moving into all sorts of areas: modeling, cosmetics and wine. When these sidelines were established he moved into the more ambitious avenues of telecommunications and airlines. The 'sky is the limit' was a limiting catch-cry to this entrepreneur who proposed flights into outer space not long after acquiring his first aircraft.

Branson's knack for turning a profit is purely entrepreneurial. He takes risks based upon sound planning and investigation but sometimes acts on gut instinct when the facts are just not available. Never one to be daunted by a challenge, Branson seems to look at any situation as being a potential opportunity. Even in failure he looks for the lesson and moves on. Under-pinning his business is a firm belief that it should be fun - if it isn't then do something else and always make sure that it is a challenge.

What does Branson look for in an entrepreneur? In his words: 'Restless questioning, the ability to ask the question 'why not?' rather than just 'why?' – and ultimately the determination to say: 'Screw it, let's do it!'. However, ultimately the entrepreneur will only succeed if he or she has good people around them and they listen to their advice. My colleagues know me as Dr Yes because I always find it hard to say 'No' to new ideas and proposals. I rely on them to guide me but ultimately I'm also prepared to trust my intuition, as long as I feel it is well informed.'

So far Dr Yes has been right more times than he has been wrong and it would seem that his intuition has been a constant companion. Branson continues to be a risk taker and eternal optimist as he pursues new and exciting ventures with the same boyish enthusiasm that started it all. Only nowadays he does so from his own island. Today, Sir Richard employs over 50,000 people that bring in an estimated £8 Billion per annum in turnover, giving him a net worth of £2 billion.

Perception

Every business person will understand the importance of using empirical analysis to solve problems. The use of cognitive approaches to problem solving is based on the principle that logic, reasoning and analysis are sound, reliable and effective. While this is true, it is only part of the story.

Psychoanalyst Carl Jung, hypothesised that a person's approach to gathering information, and subsequently making a decision, is based upon the way in which they perceive the world. He categorised people as being basically "intuitive" versus "sensate" in relation to information gathering, and "thinking" versus "feeling" in their approach to decision making. We now know that our brain functions in primarily a creative capacity or logical one – often described as right and left brain tendencies respectively.

Men (primarily 'left brain') have tended to consider the softer skill of intuition to be less effective in the area of management because of their predisposition to using analysis. Generally speaking, women are more likely to use non-cognitive processes such as sensation and feeling to make a decision, while men tend to use cognitive processes such as observation and logic. However, studies have shown conclusively that the application of logic, analysis and reasoning are not the only bases for decision-making and that intuition is in fact just as valid.

Intuition is now widely regarded as an essential basis for strategic thinking. Although some evidence exists to demonstrate that there is a clear difference between the way that men and women make decisions, neither process is right or wrong. The experience of many entrepreneurs and chief executives is revealing that 'gut feel' is sometimes the main reason for their final decision and increasingly relied upon in situations of limited time or empirical evidence.

We all process information differently. There is no single style of leadership, just as there is no single style of human being. What makes you unique is your ability to apply your beliefs and feelings to different circumstances. Several people may come to the same conclusion based upon the facts before them but that does not mean that it is right. An outcome may be justified on the basis of profitability in a business context in the short term but if the decision is ethically flawed then it may in fact be the wrong decision in the long term. While management texts advocate using certain techniques, and management consultants advise following tried and tested models, in the end decision-making is a personal thing. You might not always come to right conclusion but at least you will feel the satisfaction that it is yours.

The big picture

Environmental astuteness and the ability to read the situation often involve having both a 'helicopter view' and the capacity to absorb many small facts quickly. The ability to see things from a 'big picture' perspective and take in data on a broad range of aspects is essential to being able to act intuitively. Contemporary authors have referred to the same approach in business, such as Malcolm Gladwell in his book 'Blink: the power of thinking without thinking'. Gladwell advocates using 'thin-slicing' or sampling a range of factors to build a composite view. He describes this as being able to 'make sense of something quickly' because 'lots of situations where careful attention to the details of a very thin slice, even for no more than a second or two, can tell us an awful lot'. If you were able to 'read the play' during a game of football or netball at school then chances are the quality is already innate. If not then looking to how others have made decisions in similar situations is an excellent starting point. The practice of sampling a number of factors and forming an overall perspective can lead to as credible a decision as having all the facts – only quicker.

Empathy

Empathy is a core skill in exercising intuition. It is the ability to apprehend the 'unspoken' situation, to sense what others feel. More importantly, it is being able to determine the 'hidden agenda' that is often at the core of another person's behaviour. While empathy might not be a word which comes to mind in relation to Napoleon he nonetheless exercised it consistently. A leader must be able to tap into the undercurrents and respond in a manner that builds rapport. This can often be very difficult where maintaining a degree of separation is also required. An understanding of the people around you engenders loyalty. The key to building understanding and empathising with those around you is 'walking the talk'. As leading proponent for 'Emotional Intelligence', Daniel Goleman, says in his books, 'empathy begins inside'. You cannot fake a feeling of being interested and you cannot fake sincerity. Leaders need to develop their level of awareness of others and read social interactions accurately in order to be able to tap into, and contribute effectively to the desired outcome. Adopting a course of action should be based upon being able to empathise with *both* your colleagues *and* your opponents.

Building commitment among people of varying beliefs and backgrounds is a difficult exercise. Nonetheless it is necessary in any new undertaking to be able to rally people and focus them on the objective. This can sometimes mean doing things that are against our nature, but in order to achieve the goal it is often necessary to be able to read the situation and adapt accordingly. As a result leaders sometime have to be chameleons. Empathy helps us overcome our own predispositions and choose a course of action that is more likely to achieve success. It is not the path of least resistance but the path of least opposition.

Summary

Intuition is our creative side, the part of us that taps into our own inner beliefs and feelings. Leadership often requires a 'sixth sense' for what needs to be done in various situations. It is not as mystical as some may believe and often arises simply from competence. Knowing when to act in a particular political climate or because of practical considerations means being able to draw on experience and the inexplicable 'gut feel' for any situation.

Central to exercising intuition is the ability to understand others and read the situation around us. This is often referred to as exercising empathy: the ability to sense the feelings of those around you. This is fundamental to understanding what they will do. When you have this ability all other human behaviour becomes far easier to understand and, more importantly, predict.

Leadership tips

Executives:
Learning to relax is not simply a stress reliever, it also facilitates intuition. Only when you relax and take time to dwell on the material before you will your intuition come to the fore.

Project managers:
Too often in these days of email and mobile phones is it easy to run the project from your desk. Build rapport and empathy by being on the scene and gaining an insight into what is 'really' happening.

Entrepreneurs:
Surround yourself with expertise that you can call upon to test what you believe. Your intuition might say one thing but experts might say another. While you can still act on what you believe having additional expertise adds a degree of reassurance.

Diligence

Nothing is more difficult, and therefore more precious, than being able to decide.

N

The maxims...

Maxim XLIV

Circumstances not permitting that a sufficiently large garrison should be left behind to defend a fortress containing hospital and stores, all measures should be taken to secure the citadel from being stormed.

Interpretation: If you cannot achieve the most desirable outcome then take steps to achieve the least worst case.

Maxim XXXIV

It should be held as a maxim to have no intervals between the different bodies forming the line of battle, unless it be done to get the enemy into a trap.

Interpretation: During any operation always ensure that your plans cover everything possible and that the procedures are robust and comprehensive. The greatest threat will come from the areas which have received the least attention.

Maxim XLIII

...the principles of field fortification have made no progress since the time of the ancients; it is even below what it was 2,000 years ago. Encouragement then should be given to officers of talent to perfect this part of their art, and to bring it to the same level.

Interpretation: Never become complacent with the way that things are or the state of things that are considered the norm.

The conditions of the position occupied should not alone decide the order of battle, which should be determined by the whole circumstances.

Interpretation: Do not confine your approach to a particular situation based solely upon your present circumstances. Consideration should be given to all circumstances and not just those within purview.

Maxim XLII

...there is no dogmatic rule in war, nor should there be one against waiting for the foe within the lines.

Interpretation: No rule should be strictly applied without considering the circumstances.

Napoleonic application

Napoleon's demand for perfection was a personal characteristic that expressed itself in his tireless endeavour to excel at everything he did. This attitude was borne out of an inherent interest in detail. It is well known that he had a superior intellect and predisposition to gathering and retain facts and figures in minute detail. His years at military school allowed him to amass a plethora of facts and figures about all of the European nations. This he was able to recite in conversation with relative ease. It was not uncommon for him to stop during a review parade and talk to a soldier that he had met on campaign, address him by his name and mentioning his town or village in conversation. He also had an enquiring mind and he would often not rest until he had all the facts available. His staff were kept constantly busy with obtaining detail that was often only necessary in a contingency situation. His passion for learning from history was also a hallmark trait that provided the base of others experience. And then there was the fervent interest in what constituted 'new technology' or 'best practice'. Most of the battlefield techniques that Napoleon employed that were considered revolutionary were in fact others ideas simply employed to perfection. Finally his knack of taking something complex and making it simple required a grasp of the 'essence' of the problem. He would often distil a situation down to a few critical elements and then focus on that which seemed to be the most probable at delivering a successful outcome. All the while the alternatives were being reconsidered in case circumstance did not agree with his estimation.

Story in a box – Napoleon the political leader

Following the coup to bring Napoleon to power the management of the country was entrusted to three 'consuls' with Napoleon being the first. As with everything that he pursued Napoleon threw himself into his position as First Consul with vigor. His previous foray into politics had been in his home town of Corsica and later through his efforts to reorganize the conquered provinces in Italy. Despite the fact that he was a soldier without any training in law or politics he still took an active part in most meetings of State. For a leader of his day to do so was irregular. The previous Bourbon kings of France took little interest in proceedings and merely ratified or rejected what was presented to them. If the proposed laws did not suit their purposes then they were simply rejected.

The legislative body in France during his time as Emperor was the Council of State. Composed of qualified lawyers and politicians this body would meet regularly to debate and enact the legislation required to run the country. Napoleon often attended these meetings and would prepare for them with an attention to detail that would rival that of its more highly trained participants. His political aides, Cambaceres and Portalis, would provide him with all of the necessary documentation so that he could be aware of the various issues under discussion. He made sure that he was thoroughly briefed on all aspects of the legislation and would often debate the points with his aides in order to clarify and identify particular issues. 'He examined each question by itself inquiring into all the authorities, times, experiences; demanding to know how it had been under ancient jurisprudence, under Louis XIV, or Frederick the Great. When a bill was presented to the First Consul, he rarely failed to ask these questions: Is this bill complete? Does it cover every case? Why have you not thought of this? Is that necessary? Is it right or useful? What is done nowadays and elsewhere?' noted Comte Pierre Louis Roederer, a notable Senator and Member of the Council of State.

Napoleon's energy and drive was overwhelming to his private secretaries. He would often dictate to several secretaries at the same time on different topics. He generally went to bed late in the evening and rose mostly mid morning (3am) on only four hours sleep. He read voraciously and would devour the proceedings of the day and research the issues to be debated in Council even before going to sleep. His bed room, like his study, was generally covered with books and articles.

His realistic approach and forthright nature was expressed through much of the legislation of the day. One of the progenitors of 'plain language' he shunned legalese and verbosity. If anything was to be created in the name of the people then he demanded that it be understandable by the same. When Senators proposed an idea and couched it in the usual bureaucratic terminology he would strip it down to its essence and ask them why they could not just say that – 'it is not an epic poem' he would sardonically assert. In a time when protocol and propriety counted for much Napoleon cut through convention like a scythe. He was a man of the people after all.

To those around him it seemed that he could do almost anything. His military talent was obvious and he had to date demonstrated amazing diplomatic abilities as well. On the back of this it seemed that he also possessed prodigious administrative talent. The establishment of the Bank of France, the reinvigoration of the economy, the enactment of innovative and far-reaching legislation, the enforcement of minimum education standards, the appeasement of the church and religious groups and so on all occurred under his governance and personal attention. No detail was too small to escape his attention and no task too big to be tackled. The First Consul seemed to be, like on the battlefield, everywhere at once.

Napoleon's planning ability and preparation for a campaign were ostensible examples of diligence. Little was left to chance. On several campaigns Napoleon was confronted with situations where his army was in an inferior position. While Napoleon was the master of the pre-emptive strike and was renowned for bringing force to bear quickly and decisively when not expected, he did so based upon sound intelligence and an understanding of the environment in which he operated.

Time and again Napoleon was faced with decisions on which the very survival of the nation was at stake. Decision-making under these circumstances placed extreme pressure upon him yet, more often than not, the results ended in triumph.

Contemporary relevance

Diligence is an often assumed quality. We all consider ourselves to be diligent in our areas of expertise. But how do we really know what it means to be diligent? What is the test of diligence? Are a small or negligible number of complaints verification that we are being diligent or is it that we are not receiving this type of feedback? The maxims identify the attribute of diligence in three particular areas: data collection, planning and decision-making. To some extent they represent a continuum: Sound decisions require effective planning while effective planning requires comprehensive data-collection. Leadership imposes an obligation to make decisions and these can only be sound if the underlying bases are in themselves sound. Diligence requires that we take steps to do all that is possible and leaving nothing to chance. Only when we have exhausted all reasonable avenues can we consider that we have acted diligently. The results

Story in a box – Sam Walton

Although largely unknown outside the United States the late Sam Walton started Wal-Mart. Today Wal-Mart is the largest retailer in the world but it was not started by a mogul intent on transforming the retail industry but a straight talking countryman from Arkansas in the countries farming belt. Walton was known for being unpretentious, conscientious and dedicated.

His career started as a store packer for JC Penny. He went on to open his own store and eventually a small chain of Walton's stores that sold the basic retail needs to local rural communities. Running Waltons was a family affair - even family vacations consisted of going to other stores to see how they did things. There wasn't much about the retail market that Walton hadn't done or didn't know by the time he reached his thirties.

In 1962 a competitor opened a discount store outside his town of Arkansas. The light bulb lit up – discount retailing! Walton decided that this was the future. His strategy was to establish a chain of discount retail stores where prices would be kept down by buying in bulk and establishing an outlet for manufacturers rather than distributors. His first step was to acquire the locations. He began to quietly buy up parcels of land between towns. Out of the way places that no one suspected as being locations for a retail store. The only critical point was that the land had to be at a major cross-road between towns. His strategy was simple: place his new stores between the largest population centres on land that was cheap, available and easy to access. He knew that even though they were out of the way people would always go looking for a bargain. After establishing his first store he chose to computer control the stock systems, well before computerised inventory and warehouse control management techniques were introduced to the retail industry. His focus on customer satisfaction was also paramount (Wal-Mart employees are encouraged every morning to answer the question 'who's number one' with 'the customer'). Stores were well lit, conveniently laid out, and appealing to shoppers. Customers were greeted on entry and assisted with their purchases. Sales staff were unusually not behind the counter. The stores themselves were huge – warehouse size. While all this may seem common-place today they were being introduced at a time when the corner store owned by a mild mannered couple dispensing flour by the scoop was still the norm. While the scale of the new stores and the layout was daunting to customers they gradually warmed to the concept and, as Walton predicted, ultimately came for the bargains.

Today Wal-Mart has become the largest retailer in the world, but not without fierce competition. The company was up against several large competitors from the outset – Kmart and Target were formed around the same time. But Walton knew the retail supply chain inside out. He knew that the key was in the profit margins of the manufacturers and distributors of goods - not in the retail component. His introduction of technology computers meant that he was the first major retailer to have product go direct from manufacturer to customer and thereby reduce inventory and distribution cost component.

In the mid eighties Walton had become the richest man in America. His stores were virtually everywhere. Despite the subsequent vilification of the Wal-Mart chain it is difficult to deny that they spawned the discount environment that is today's modern shopping experience. The elements of the retail business that were considered revolutionary during the sixties and the seventies are today commonplace. None of it seemed revolutionary to Walton, it was what needed to be done. He knew his market and he did whatever was necessary to ensure that the business would succeed.

Diligence is applying yourself to the best of your abilities through industrious and dedicated attention to the task at hand. Leadership provides an example for others to follow - people are always inspired by commitment and dedication.

Diligence can be exercised through having a 'big picture' perspective and seeking out better ways of doing things. The modern corporate environment imposes due diligence to ensure that a process has been followed accurately, which should be advocated by anyone in a leadership position.

Diligence is not simply about doing things with an obsessive attitude. It is more about the manner in which you approach a situation. It is apparent in Napoleon's character that he possessed five traits that can readily be identified as relevant to almost any leaders career:

- A keen interest in detail
- An enquiring mind
- A passion for learning from history
- A desire to seek out alternatives
- An ability to take the complex and make it simple

It is the application of this approach in the modern business context that demonstrates leadership.

Data collection

Being responsible for making bad decisions is one of the obligations of leadership. To allay this possibility exercising diligence is key. One of the best means of supporting any decision is to have as much data as possible to rely upon. This may sound obvious but in general, most people make decisions by firstly trying to reduce the scope of the problem. This process is known as 'bounded rationality' whereby a person will seek to limit the number of choices by reducing the array of available information either because of external constraints, such as time, or internal constraints, such as intellectual capacity. Ultimately this approach is sought to make the process of deciding easier. The end result is that sound decisions become a little hit or miss. Leadership imposes the almost opposite approach. Seeking out additional information so that the decision can be made in light of as much data as possible is difficult and demanding. This quality has been identified as an essential component of 'executive intelligence'. In Dr Justin Menkes Book 'Executive Intelligence' the ability to take in large amounts of information and process it (with or without the aid of sub-ordinates) is one of the key indicators of whether a senior executive has what it takes to succeed. The ability demonstrates that the person possesses an analytical mind of great capacity. These attributes have always differentiated the superior intellect from the mediocre. It is also not a matter of having these qualities or not as they can be developed as long as the will to improve is present.

The quality of diligence is exercised when we follow the more difficult path. The exigencies of time may not always make this possible but that is generally more an issue of planning. Only when you are armed with a comprehensive picture of the situation are you likely to make the best of many possible decisions, rather than the best of a limited number. Leadership imposes the responsibility of analysing the information available and then seeking more.

Planning

Diligence in the planning process is essential for achieving the desired outcome. It goes without saying that planning requires that as much as possible be done to ensure that the plans are as sound as they can possibly be. The question becomes: how do we know that we have exercised diligence in the planning process? If we have followed the methodology and completed all the base documentation have we not discharged our obligation? Not really. Diligence is not just about following a process but about the approach that is taken within that process. We have already discussed the requirement to expand our data gathering approach to include as wide an array as possible. Employing techniques such as brainstorming, workshops, questionnaires and so on are ways of ensuring that we have considered as much as possible in formulating our plans.

Project managers are often called upon to make estimates about the duration of a project without having the 'full picture'. Consultation with key stakeholders and reliance upon historical and personal expertise are generally the approach utilised to propose a schedule of activity and resultant project duration. Competent project managers will go one step further and use a weighted average system to determine the duration of activities. The weighted average technique is based on an average of three component – the 'most likely' duration of the activity (based upon historical data and experience), the optimistic likelihood of completion (generally the customers perception) and the pessimistic likelihood of completion. The technique takes these three estimates and then averages them according to the following formula:

$$\frac{O + 4ML + P}{6}$$

mathematical estimating can be more time consuming it is far better than the usual 'guesstimates'. The difference being that there is a greater degree of traceability in the calculation and a much broader consideration of factors.

The use of similar techniques will mean that any plan will have greater credibility. There are an array of various techniques to make any aspect of planning more efficacious. Leadership imposes the responsibility to be aware of these and ensure that the necessary steps have been taken to have plans based upon not only the best available data but the most rigorous analysis as well.

Decision-making

We are rarely provided with all of the information that is required to make the 'best' decision. Ironically it is rare to know the 'best' decision with any certainty yet we somehow intuitively always seem to know the 'worst' decision that we could make. A good or bad decision is highly subjective. The best or worst decision is often a matter of opinion after the event. The objective in decision-making in some circumstances is not to make the 'best' decision but to choose between the extremes of best and worst cases. Leaders are often expected to make 'good' decisions that result in the best outcome but diligence in decision-making is about choosing between the array of likely possibilities in coming to a conclusion. The 'best' decision may not always have the most optimal outcome.

In any environment there are competing interests. A leader is required to look at the various competing interests and decide upon the course that delivers the most desirable outcome. One area which demonstrates the range of possible decisions that can be made in a given scenario is the prisoners dilemma in Games theory. Games theory advocates that there is always a dominant strategy where any party will be trying to obtain the most beneficial outcome for themselves. Where two competing interest are involved the dominant strategy will result in the selection of the least worst case result. The prisoners dilemma is a situation where two prisoners can either decide to confess to a crime and receive a lower sentence or collude and deny the allegations. The dominant strategy, that which delivers the best outcome, is for each party is to collude and remain silent on the charges. Doing so may mean achieving the lowest sentence due to insufficient evidence. Their dilemma is that if one of them confesses while the other remains silent on the allegations then the party confessing will obtain a lighter sentence and the one that remains silent will carry the full and maximum burden for the crime. Alternatively if they both confess (neither knowing whether the other has) then they will obtain a lower sentence than if they had remained silent and given their accomplice the opportunity to confess. The scenarios can be displayed in the following table as the likely outcomes for their actions.

	Prisoner A	
	Confess	Silent
Confess	Prisoner A 5 years / Prisoner B 5 years	Prisoner B 6 months / Prisoner A 10 years
Silent	Prisoner B 10 years / Prisoner A 6 months	Prisoner A 18 months / Prisoner B 18 months

Prisoner B

The resultant matrix of decision making can therefore be regarded as being made up not just of the best and the worst case.

Least best case	Best case
Worst case	Least worst case

The best case decision is therefore only worthwhile for one party. The same applies for the worst case decision. When two competing parties adopt the same strategy then the result is either the least best case (if they chose to adopt a dominant strategy and defect) or the least worst case (if they chose to not adopt a dominant strategy and co-operate). Diligence is exercised when we don't just consider the best or the worst case but the situations between. It is often that the in-between decisions result in the 'best' decision when competing interests are involved.

The underlying principles of the prisoner's dilemma are present in almost every decision-making process. Strong leadership doesn't only look at the extremes but the range of options in between. The Cuban missile crisis was a salient example of this in practice. President Kennedy was faced with one of the most daunting decisions of any leader in modern history – that of precipitating a nuclear world war. The military in the US advocated that the best decision was to pre-emptively attack due to the presence of nuclear weapons so close to the US mainland. The alternative was to do nothing and wait to be attacked and possibly risk annihilation. Kennedy's decision was one of forcing Kruschev to back down by removing the nuclear weapons in Cuba. If they did not then the US would be forced to invade and that would most likely cause a retaliatory strike upon the US. The worst case was nuclear war - annihilation. The best case was to invade and achieve total victory in one fell swoop. Between these two extremes existed the possibility of the mutual removal of nuclear arms. The resultant engagement in brinkmanship resulted in the least worst case, that is, the US were forced to sacrifice some of their own strategic nuclear arms deployments in exchange for the USSR removing the threat from Cuba. To the military the outcomes was anathema but the risk posed from the 'best' decision was simply too high.

This type of analysis can be applied to any decision where there are competing interests. It can be valuable regardless of whether a decision between internal competing interests are involved or where external competing interest are involved. Hotelling theory advocates that two competitors are better off co-operating and sharing the market rather than adopting tactics to seek a market advantage. Even though the dominant strategy is for both organisations to take as much of the market as possible they are in the best situation when they accept the least worst case and share the market equally. Considering each parties agenda, the trade-offs and the possible results is the basis of exercising diligence in the decision making process.

Summary

Leaders are relied upon to make sound, rational and justifiable decisions. Inevitably there will always be situations where you will be faced with less than optimal choices. Considerable personal effort and courage are required to make decisions that involve undesirable outcomes. Diligence involves possessing the tenacity to ensure that nothing has been overlooked. Without this ability you are unlikely to have the capacity to make the decisions required of a highly effective leader. In the final analysis all decisions are ultimately a balancing act of competing interests. There are no finite principles that determine the 'best' decision - only the most sound.

It is a signal trait of good leadership to always seek out better ways to achieve results. Leader who demonstrate this capability are often sought out in any sphere. While there are particular traits that demonstrate a proclivity for being diligent the act of seeking out as much data as possible, planning comprehensively and making decisions with regard to all of the competing interests and outcomes is diligence in practice. Ultimately you are held accountable for any decision made as leader so it is incumbent to ensure that everything possible has been done to be satisfied that it is the justifiable. Making the best decision should not always be the aim but making a decision with the most desirable outcome under the circumstances.

Leadership tips

Executives:
In any activity that has political or public consequences it pays to bring in the experts. Always keep an eye on the legal, environmental and ethical requirements for any process that imposes accountability.

Project managers:
Following a project management methodology is not just about joining the dots. A methodology is there to ensure that all things that need to be done are done. Leaving parts out to save time or because they don't seem to be relevant is courting danger.

Entrepreneurs:
Know the environment and the surrounding legislation in any new venture before starting out – regulations, licensing requirements, environmental obligations, zoning and so on will all have an effect on the success of any enterprise.

Judgement

From the sublime to the ridiculous is but a step.

N

The maxims...

Maxim LXXIX

The first principle of a commander-in-chief is to observe clearly what he does, to see if he has all the means of surmounting any obstacle the enemy may place in his way, and if he has made up his mind to do all to overcome those obstacles.

Interpretation: See every situation without distraction or personal motivation, determine what needs to be done and decide on the best means of achieving it.

Maxim XIV

...In mountain warfare the assailant always has the disadvantage. Even in offensive warfare in the open field the great secret consists of defensive combats, and in obliging the enemy to attack

Interpretation: Understand the surrounding conditions in which you will engage with a competitor. Be aware of as much as possible about your adversary. Adopt a strategy that is appropriate to the circumstances.

Maxim XVI

It is an approved maxim of war, never to do what the enemy wishes you to do, for this reason alone, that he desires it. A field of battle, therefore, which he has previously studied and reconnoitred, should be avoided, and double care should be taken where he has had time to fortify and entrench. One consequence deducible from this principle is, never to attack a position in front which you can gain by turning.

Interpretation: Never do what your opponent desires you to do. Choose the environment and conditions that you wish to operate in or under – do not allow others to dictate the conditions. If possible avoid situations which pose unacceptable risk, if not then always have in place a strategy to counteract any disadvantageous eventualities.

Maxim LXXXV

To a talented general who has to think out, propose, and execute everything by himself, good judgment and a solid mind are necessary.

Interpretation: If you have the responsibility to plan and carry out an operation then sound judgement and a strong mind are essential.

Maxim XCVII

The rules of war demand that a division of an army should avoid fighting alone a whole army which has already scored success.

Interpretation: Regardless of your own perceived strength know your opponent before taking them on – especially when they have a record of success or competitive advantage.

Napoleonic application

Napoleon exercised judgement in both military and political affairs through careful consideration of facts before him. He approached every situation with an awareness of what could go wrong and he also planned for how to counteract it. His study of campaigns of previous military leaders, and an alertness to the role of chance gave him an insight into how his opponents might act. On this basis, Napoleon always elected to occupy a strong defensive position to launch a 'well reasoned' attack. He would often direct his Marshals to select a strong defensive capable of seizing the initiative at the same time. He was cautious yet decisive with an uncanny capacity for knowing the right moment to act. Operations were a matter of fine balance between strength in defence yet remaining formidable in attack.

Story in a box – The central position

The 'central position' was a favourite in Napoleon's tactics. This was not simply a matter of obtaining a central point on the battlefield as it was very likely that in doing so his army could be surrounded. The trick was in understanding the terrain, timing, troop movements, and the juncture where his opponent was likely to converge or diverge. Napoleon was able to determine these things from a preternatural understanding of terrain and an almost prescient awareness of an opposing force's weakest point. He would then direct his forces to converge on the weak point and exploit that position to attack their flanks or rear.

There was nothing new in this approach. Divide and conquer was a favourite tactic used to superb effect by the ancient Romans – notably Julius Caesar. Its success depended primarily on interposing his army between the opposing forces and separating them. Napoleon did so on the battlefield by having approximately two thirds of his force attack approximately half of an opposing army with the remaining third pinning the other half of the opposing force so as to prevent them coming to the aid of the besieged. When the attacking force gained the upper hand some of them would be despatched to pursue the fleeing forces, while the remainder would join the 'pinning' force to increase the attack on their opponents. Additional troops coming into this environment had the effect of appearing as reinforcements and morale was consequently affected on both sides.

This central position was used time and again as a strategic positioning for the French army. First used effectively in the Italian campaign Napoleon continued to refine the approach in future battles, but the principle always remained the same - take control of the ground between two opposing forces and seek to defeat one before the other could come to its rescue. In the Battle of Rivoli, during the first Italian campaign, Napoleon was outnumbered and in danger of being surrounded by the converging Austrian forces. His dilemma was to either maintain the siege of Mantua (to obtain victory and access to Milan) or abandon the siege and turn to meet his converging opponents before they could unite. Not only was the siege abandoned but Napoleon's forces took up locations to be able to defeat the opposition as independent units before they could unite in force.

In the Prussian campaign it was Napoleon's strategy to move first against the Austrians to knock them out before the Russians could reinforce them. The Battle of Austerlitz saw Napoleon drive a wedge between the two opposing forces, primarily through deception to effectively cut them off from reinforcing each other. The objective in this and all subsequent engagements was to divide the opposing force and overpower a small force rather than a large one. It was not as simple as it sounded and often relied upon extremely good co-ordination of the different corps. Through this technique Napoleon's armies were often able to defeat larger forces.

Despite his predisposition to attack whenever the opportunity presented itself he did not slavishly succumb to any particular tactic without sound reasoning – calling upon the experience gained from prior battles or that of the past military leaders he had studied. Napoleon was also the master of 'moving the goalposts' forcing others to operate as he desired. His preference was to fight on ground of his own choosing, or dupe the enemy into going for a perceived advantage that was in fact a well laid trap. One of the key lessons from Napoleon's campaigns was his attitude to be proactive and obtain as much information as possible prior to embarking upon a particular venture. Information provided the means to plan, act decisively and be proactive. Rapidity of movement and a well executed strategy often stymied the efforts of two or more opposing armies. Judgement was key. Napoleon looked for the 'hinge' in battle which came about through an understanding of the manner in which the opposing force would need to approach and then act to pre-empt the situation. Time and time again Napoleon's enemies were confounded by what appeared to be overwhelming opposition but was in fact the exploitation of their weakness.

Contemporary relevance

Sound judgement is a quality that all leaders must have. But what is 'sound judgement' or 'good judgement'? Whose yardstick is used to assess whether judgement is 'good' or 'sound'? Judgement is a subjective phenomenon. What will be deemed good judgement to one person is regarded less positively by another. You may be the most competent person in your field but others may still regard your judgement as being a little 'off'. The consequence being that you are not quite as successful as you would have hoped. Doors don't seem to open as easily despite your expertise.

Judgement is related to our sense of reasoning rather than competence or pure intellect. It is based on our interpretation of the surrounding circumstances and shares more in common with intuition; relying upon our own experience, values and ability to apprehend the context in which decisions and actions are taken. Good judgement springs from our ability to be impartial and objective. Taking in facts and processing them without colour is essential. Judgement should be without bias and be rational and objective.

Story in a box – Wendelin Weideking

One of the simple rules in business is that if you have a successful product don't mess with it. Seemingly obvious advice but German sports car company, Porsche, decided to do the opposite. Known primarily as a manufacturer of rear engined motor vehicles, culminating in the production of the legendary 911, the eighties saw a series of front-engined vehicles introduced to an ever more sophisticated and well healed motoring public. Porsche's venerated mainstay, the rear-engined '911' was being phased out to make way for a 'new' and invigorated model range. *Porschephiles* and car enthusiasts everywhere were dumbfounded. Porsche's reputation had in no small part been built upon the classic 911.

When the eighties bubble burst so did Porsches fortunes, with high production costs for a burgeoning model range, and dwindling sales. One of the world's greatest sports car manufacturers was on the ropes and almost out of business by 1991 with accumulated losses of over $US90 million.

In 1992 Wendelin Weideking was appointed production manager for Porsche AG. He observed that while the Company had great pride in its motor vehicles they were hopelessly out of date in relation to modern manufacturing techniques. A legacy of hand-built cars remained as a homage to the days when the best vehicles were made by craftsmen. Wiedeking knew that this attitude could not remain in the face of the Japanese automotive juggernaut. With these things in mind Weideking proposed that Porsche revert back to its mainstay product, the 911, and modernize the production process.

At the time this attitude seemed diametrically opposed to the philosophy of the company which was founded on innovation and craftsmanship. As a consequence he faced strong internal opposition from almost every quarter. In substance he was advocating a one product company! The sales distribution network was horrified. They relied upon new products to tantalize customers and with the already dwindling sales how could they increase business on the back of an ageing design. Morale on the factory floor also dropped as many in the production environment realised that rationalisation meant job losses.

Line management were retrenched, production processes shut down and distribution channels rationalized. Porsche went back to being a one product company - based around a rather expensive product at that. Weideking wanted to consolidate Porsche's position and eradicate the accumulating cost from product lines that were not performing. The 911 became four different versions of the one thing with new identities - the Carerra, Cabriolet, Targa and Turbo. Customers liked the new, more ergonomically designed product. Sales started to rise with the focus on quality and image.

On the back of the product rationalization Wiedeking proposed that Porsche now introduce a model that harked back to its halcyon days. A model that said that Porsche was about making true sports cars based on a tradition of uncompromising excellence. At the same time the vehicle needed to be more affordable to usher in a new wave of Porsche buyers. Customers remained dubious - they had to be convinced that the 'new' Porsche was not some low cost ruse like the unloved front-engined 924 had been. The new model had to invigorate Porsche's image and win new blood to the marque while at the same time linking the company to its past. The 'Boxster' was born to an expectant motoring industry and sold as a 'true Porsche'. The engine was kept in the rear (mid-mounted). It had all the right looks yet was almost half the cost of the Carerra. Receiving rave reviews the Boxster was welcomed worldwide not only as a true Porsche but an outstanding sports-car.

Porsche now had a model range with a distinct and recognizable look; from the market entry Boxster through to the supercar Carerra GT. With production costs down and market acceptance up Porsche was literally back in the driving seat. Efficiencies in the supply chain and on the factory floor saw costs drop. Porsche became so good at its new approach that its design personnel started consulting to other firms such as Harley Davidson and Airbus to improve their operations. This became the new corporate culture: if a part of Porsches operation was idle it went looking for work elsewhere.

The process of turning around Porsche's fortunes was risky but essentially based upon sound judgment and an appreciation for what the market wanted, and what the Company could achieve. Porsche today enjoys an enviable position making arguably the world's best sports cars for both on and off the road - and the family resemblance across the range is unmistakable.

Judgement in the modern business context can derive four basic principles from the maxims:
- Preparation
- Timing
- Opportunism
- Understanding context

Preparation

The need to plan and be prepared is paramount to exercising sound judgement. This is not only reflected in Napoleon's maxims but in the manner in which he approached every campaign. The quality of preparation has been amplified in recent management literature by Warren Bennis and Noel Tichy in their book 'Judgement: How winning leaders make great calls'. The authors identify that judgement is, in a nutshell, 'a process of preparation ..., making the judgment call, making execution happen, and learning and continuously adjusting after the call is made.[3]' The key here is preparation – having a plan. Every situation that requires a particular outcome needs a plan of action. It can be as simple as a time management plan for your day or as complex as a project plan for a major undertaking, but planning is something that needs to be done whenever there are resources, uncertainties, commitments or deliverables involved. Sound planning is key to being able to respond to uncertainty and change, and be in control despite the circumstances around you.

Preparing for any venture and gathering information is essential to gaining an insight into the situation. Our perceptions are sometimes in conflict with reality when we do not have all the facts. Your own beliefs, values and biases often colour facts. A conclusion based upon a series of 'facts' can sometimes be as much about your perception of the meaning of these facts. We are all aware of the rubbery nature of statistics and that data can be processed in various ways to deliver different results. To minimise the inappropriate interpretation of facts it is important to understand your own biases and be aware to situations when it could colour your own judgement. Does the information that you receive mean what you think it means, or does it have some completely different meaning, or indeed no significance at all?

Timing

Probably one of the most desirable and sought after qualities in any sphere is that of someone with a sense of timing. Deciding when to act and choosing the most propitious moment is sometimes the difference between success and failure. Making a decision to act at a particular point in time might sometimes seem a matter of luck to most but is more likely to be perceived as good judgement. Quite often the desire to act can be compelling because of a need to produce results. This is where restraint needs to be exercised and strength of character to oppose those that may impatiently want to move immediately. While action is important it is far more important to take action at the right moment. Decision-making is not just about being decisive but being able to decide when it counts.

---

[3] Harvard Business Review 'Does Judgement trump experience', Jim Haskett, January 2008.

Of greater concern for leaders is how to ensure that decisions are implemented at the right time. There are several aspects of this issue. We can rely upon those around us to advise and then make a judgement call based upon all of the information or we can use our own intuition or indeed a combination of the two. While timing can be progressively improved through experience it is often required throughout our careers and not simply when we have obtained the necessary experience. There is probably no simple explanation as to how a sense of timing is developed. You might be a typically decisive person and make decisions without qualms but at the same time be seen as being impulsive and impetuous. On the other hand you may have a consultative and collaborative approach that forestalls your decision-making and marks you as having a tendency to prevaricate. Either way knowing your style and being aware your decision-making style will assist in making sure that when the moment comes there is everything possible going for it.

Opportunism

Opportunism seems to have nasty connotations in the business environment. Taking advantage of opportunities seems to be on par with taking advantage of others. Contrary to this belief opportunism is being on the look out for a beneficial advantage. This may on occasion call for the exploitation of a weakness but regardless of the ethics involved a leader should always be ready to seize an opportunity.

Proposing change and moving people in a new direction is fundamental to leadership. Organisations need to change to improve or maintain their competitive advantage. The enemy of any organisation is complacency. Complacency can occur far more surreptitiously than we might imagine. Management can become lured into believing that everything is operating as it should; people are following procedures and the organisation is doing what it should be doing. Unless an organisation is exploring new and better ways of doing business then they are in a state of stagnation and ultimately decline. Good leadership means constantly pushing the boundaries to improve. Maintaining the status quo is simply supporting inertia. Moving from a state of stagnation to innovation require double effort - firstly overcoming the inertia and then moving in the right direction. If an organisation is constantly ready to seize a new opportunity then it will always be ready to respond to change.

Understanding context

Your personal style or preferred way of doing things may be a contributor to the way you assess and interpret information. For example, if you are predominantly aggressive or suspicious by nature then you are quite likely to react differently to information than someone who has a different persuasion. One should always have confidants that can bring a different perspective to the table. Being aware of your own style and taking steps to keep your innate predispositions in check is important to exercising sound judgement.

Sometimes it helps to just sit back and ask "so what"? Any information should be regarded with circumspection. As the old adage goes - 'believe half of what you read and none of what you hear'. Your judgement will be greatly assisted by testing your decisions against the views of others. Leadership ultimately requires you to take risks and act. This makes the objective consideration of information even more critical. Use as many resources as you can to reach a conclusion but in the end weigh up the pros and cons, dig deep into yourself and decide.

Summary

Sound judgement is underpinned by competence and experience. Possessing the skills and knowledge in your position is a base expectation, but the way in which you make decisions is an indication of your judgement. Judgement manifests itself as being cautious, circumspect or prudent. An awareness of the ramifications of your actions is necessary to guide decision-making and come to a cogent conclusion. The ability to make the best decision and take the most appropriate course of action under the circumstances is imposed as part of the responsibility of leadership.

Leadership requires the ability to deal with people and collect as much information as possible before deciding on the course of action. The importance of obtaining information from a variety of sources, and determining the credibility of those sources, will assist in establishing a clear picture of the total environment. Any intelligence should be tested against various sources and considered carefully before acting. Good judgement means making use of all available means at your disposal to achieve the end required. This may sometimes involve employing traditional means in unique ways - the opportunist will always outwit the gullible. Making use of the strategic resources that you have available but always ensuring that they remain well supported is a delicate balancing act. Ultimately judgement is about making use of the things around you to achieve the most desirable outcome.

Leadership tips

Executives:

Know where your organisation fits into the big picture and know how it will handle current trends, market cycles and political impacts.

Project managers:

While it is necessary to focus on all aspects of a project it is also fundamental that the problematic components receive sufficient, and often disproportionate, attention. Don't let the problem areas hijack a well planned project.

Entrepreneurs:

Research any new venture through as many sources as possible. Sometimes the least obvious location will provide information that could make an initiative unviable.

Foresight

If I always appear prepared, it is because before entering an undertaking I have meditated long and have foreseen what might occur.

N

The maxims...

Maxim II

In forming the plan of a campaign, it is requisite to foresee everything the enemy may do, and to be prepared with the necessary means to counteract it. Plans of campaign may be modified ad infinitum according to the circumstances, the genius of the General, the character of the troops, and the features of the country

Interpretation: Being able to anticipate what might happen and having an approach in place to deal with that contingency is essential in planning. Planning should be a fluid exercise and you should always be prepared to adapt to the surrounding circumstances.

Maxim LIV

Artillery should always be placed in the most advantageous positions, and as far in front of the line of cavalry and infantry, without compromising the safety of the guns, as possible. Field batteries should command the whole country round from the level of the platform. They should on no account be masked on the right and left, but have free range in every direction.

Interpretation: Regardless of whether the current circumstances appear benign you should always be in a position to act and take advantage of any opportunity. Approach any situation as if it is the real thing.

Maxim XCV

War is made up of accidents, and although bound to follow general principles, a general ought not to lose from sight anything which may enable him to profit from these accidents; it is a characteristic of talent. In war there is but one favourable moment: the great thing is to seize it.

Interpretation: Take advantage of any opportunity that presents itself - the unexpected can be as fortuitous as it is dangerous.

Napoleonic application

Napoleon was particularly strong in mathematics. One of the strands of mathematics that was to form his fundamental appreciation of risk was probability theory[4]. Probability analysis imbues a very clinical attitude in those that appreciate the role of chance. Napoleon was not opposed to taking risks, in fact he thrived on risk taking. He would often command a tactical manoeuvre to destabilise his opponent and then assess the result. This would then determine his next manoeuvre and so on – just like a probability decision tree. It was on this basis that Napoleon would take calculated risks to tip the balance: 'it is the one drop that causes the cup to overflow'.

In planning a campaign Napoleon would consider the permutations of certain action and assign a relative probability to them. Planning and preparation was on the basis of what might happen and what was known. No detail was too insignificant. On the battle-field possessing the right information, weighing up the risks and having the necessary contingency plans in place were all important to the achieving victory.

Story in a box – The Battle of Austerlitz (1805)

During the early years of the nineteenth century the European powers suspicion of France grew in proportion to its imperialist intentions. The planned invasion of England and the expansion of French interests into Italy and the Mediterranean were seen as major threats. Financed by English funds Austria and Russia were encouraged to invade France to restore the status quo and cork the revolutionary foment. Upon hearing of the planned invasion Napoleon acted quickly. With characteristic determination the *Grande Armée* was mobilised to confront the Austrian army, well before they could meet up with the Russians and reach the French border. The Austrians were effectively surrounded at the Austrian town of Ulm ending in the capitulation of a significant proportion of the Austrian army before they had any effect on France or its interests.

The euphoria of victory gave way to trepidation as the French found themselves seriously outnumbered facing an 80,000 strong Russian army, bolstered by remnants from the Austrian army with severely stretched supply lines. French communications stretched from Vienna to Paris, making resupply impossible and posing the problem of being cut-off by the Russians.

In order to defeat his opponent Napoleon's strategy relied upon the Russians behaving in a predictable and manageable manner. He knew he was outnumbered and so decided to drive a wedge between the approaching force – 'divide and conquer' his opponents with his favourite tactic of pining and envelopment. The only

---

[4] The study of random occurrences of events used to define the degree of certainty, or uncertainty, of an event occurring.

way to do this was to lure them into a situation where his inferior numbers could be used their greatest effect.

On the morning of the battle near the town of Austerlitz Napoleon deliberately vacated the high ground known as the Pratzen Heights. He then agreed to meet with the Russian emissary to discuss terms for ending the conflict. During this meeting he feigned fear and confusion. The overall picture to the Russian and Austrian commanders was that the French were not confident and that Napoleon had committed a grave tactical error. While the taste of the Austrian's defeat at Ulm was still palpable they knew that Napoleon had over stretched his forces. The Russian commander, Czar Alexander, felt confident that victory was in their hands.

To further bolster the confidence of his opponents Napoleon deliberately feigned weakness in his left flank. As expected the battle commenced with the Russians attacking that flank. To their surprise the attack became bogged down as it drew in more and more men. Napoleon had concealed reinforcements making the conflict more intractable than expected. To meet the demand Russian troops were diverted from the centre. At the same time the occupation of the Pratzen Heights saw further Russian troops moving in the other direction. What resulted was a diverging army. Russian troops were moving to the left and the right and thus denuding their centre. This violated the principle of concentration of force and exposed a weakness that Napoleon had planned to exploit. The Russian and Austrian commanders looked on in vain as they saw what was about to happen. Concealed French reinforcements emerged to infiltrate the widening gap. The French were now interposed between the separated Russian army with one side pinned down and the other flank seriously outnumbered. Reinforcements were needed urgently by the Russians from the Pratzen Heights. The high ground was always going to be the key but it needed to be taken with minimum forces – all Napoleon had left. Russian troops were diverted from the Heights to repel the incursions.

Standing on a hill observing the movement of the enemy troops Napoleon asked Marshall Soult how long he would take to recapture the Heights. 'Twenty minutes, Sire' came the reply. Napoleon responded 'We will wait another quarter of an hour'. Napoleon knew the moment when the high ground would have sufficiently few troops on it to facilitate its recapture while at the same time not allowing enough enemy troops from the high ground to threaten his right flank. Soult was despatched and with bayonets fixed his division marched up the hill under cover of fog. As the approaching French lines emerged the Russians panicked and fled.

With the high ground captured the French could now swing around and attack the rear of the Russian army. As more and more French soldiers swept into the beleaguered Russian formations from their concealed positions resistance crumbled. The Russian army was now effectively surrounded and retreated in complete disarray.

Napoleon's victory at Austerlitz has been lauded as perhaps his greatest. Utilising every means at his disposal the combined Russian and Austrian armies behaved exactly as anticipated. Manipulation, preparation and deception were all used to outstanding effect.

Contemporary relevance

Foresight is not about telling the future - there are no magical qualities about it. It is also not about having all the answers but it does mean having enough knowledge of the environment and people around you to be able to act. If you don't have the answer then call on those that might. Expertise is not just about possessing knowledge but being able to access the knowledge of those that have what you need.

The engagement of strategic planners and risk advisors can provide insight into what you need or focus your attention on in particular areas. External parties may help in identifying elements that are not immediately obvious. All too often being close to the 'coal face' diverts our attention from being able to think strategically and rise above the day to day issues.

Foresight can be exercised through several common business modelling system. Trend analysis, simulation testing, sensitivity analysis, forecasting and some of these techniques. These methods can be built upon to improve your abilities to predict and pre-empt. Most of us use these techniques and are aware of their significance but how often do we actually apply them? This is a critical consideration in both the planning and execution phases of any strategy.

Story in a box –Bill Gates

In the late seventies the computer industry was dominated by IBM. Large companies had large mainframes, small companies had mid range computers and everyone else had nothing. Software was written in house and mainframes were largely leased from large computer corporations. Computerisation was prohibitively expensive, highly centralized and technically specialised. It would seem that nothing would ever change this paradigm.

Despite the status quo a revolution in computing was underway with the first 'micro' computers emerging in the US. Crude and cheap, these devices were purely hobbyist territory. Like their mainframe counterparts they also needed software to run. Into this new world came two entrepreneurial programmers named Bill Gates and Paul Allen. Allen suggested that they should perhaps contact the manufacturer of one of these new 'micro' computers and offer to write software for it. A short time later Gates and Allen established a small business called Micro-Soft and produced the computer language BASIC. The new language spread with amazing speed. There was obviously a market for microcomputer software. On the back of this success they began writing other software and selling it to the other micro computer manufacturers. More microcomputer firms emerged and Micro-soft business grew.

And grew. By the early eighties the micro-computer industry had arrived. Home enthusiasts and small businesses saw the potential and business software emerged to make them increasingly effective. In the meantime IBM was caught on the back foot. Not wanting to entertain the threat from something so 'powerless' they had all but ignored the presence of these toy computers. But their customers could not be ignored and so, reluctantly, they entered the micro-computer market with the IBM Personal Computer (PC).

Like every other microcomputer manufacturer IBM needed an operating system and software for their computer. Not wanting to enter the micro-computer software market they turned to the fledgling Micro-Soft to provide them with an operating system. Gates and his partner Paul Allen saw the opportunity but didn't have a solution. But Allen knew someone that did and so purchased the rather inauspiciously named 86DOS from a local competitor. They re-badged it PC-DOS for the IBM PC. So as to have a share of the growing microcomputer market Micro-Soft licensed the software to IBM. Gates knew that other manufacturers would simply copy the IBM architecture and that these devices would also need an operating system. IBM didn't consider the PC a threat to their established business so simply requested an exclusive licence for PC DOS but left the copyright vested in Micro-Soft. The clone market exploded and, once again, Microsoft was there with a version of DOS for everyone else – MS DOS.

As the clone market took over business became more demanding of greater software functionality. The Apple Macintosh had demonstrated the ease of use and simplicity of the graphical user interface and other manufacturers started to follow suit. Gates saw that the graphical user interface was the future. Following a visit to the Xerox Palo Alto Research Centre, where a "windows" operating system was demonstrated, Gates set Micro-Soft the new task of creating what has today become the dominant operating system – Windows. By the nineties Microsoft had definitely established a niche with their operating system and a range of products that integrated with Windows offering word processing, spreadsheets, presentation products and so forth.

When the internet arrived Gates foresaw its significance and sent a clarion call to the organisation that it would be the single biggest threat to the survival of the company. Microsoft quickly created a web browser product (Internet Explorer) to take on the dominant Netscape Navigator. Once again Microsoft prevailed and today is estimated to have a 90% share of the world's software market. Shortly before retiring from Microsoft Gates once again foreshadowed the significance of the internet and attempted to steer the company to acquire the internet search engine.

Imagination

A vivid imagination is often a powerful ally in decision making. Being observant and always questioning the status quo will elicit information that may be critical to the final decision. Intuition and foresight are powerful allies and are fundamentally based upon an understanding of the past, an awareness of our present environment and an appreciation of the impact of our decisions for the future. Some have referred to this approach as the use of 'creative imaging' to be able to appreciate the range of possibilities that may exist. Imaging a situation that could occur sounds childish but it has also marked the emergence of some of the most significant technology in history.

Contingency planning

Foresight is a characteristic that helps us plan. The creation of contingency plans is a particularly good example of looking at the current situation and imaging what might go wrong. Even though this type of planning takes time it should always be performed for any high risk undertaking. Any executive that has responsibility for multi-million dollar investments and implementations should take into account the consequences of something not going according to plan, otherwise they should accept the consequences. This aspect of responsibility is also a result of foresight – if you fail to act in advance then be prepared to accept the consequences.

Risk

To enter into any situation where the outcome is unknown (and be honest with yourself – how many outcomes in business are really known?) requires an assessment of the different scenarios and their outcomes. An appreciation of probability theory is a good start to understanding the fundamentals of being able to determine what *might* happen and understand the likelihood of its happening. The assessment of the likelihood then leads on to an appreciation of the consequences of any course of action. These concepts underpin what is commonly known as risk assessment.

Risk assessment is fundamentally about exercising foresight. Employing this technique usually involves brain-storming with people of differing expertise to determine the probability of various occurrences. The process provides the means to predict the possibilities of adverse outcomes and enables the formation of contingency plans (often referred to as mitigation strategies). Conducting a risk assessment requires that it be performed with the same attention to detail as if the risk has materialised. Being able to 'foresee' the situation is critical. It is also necessary to be politically and organisationally connected so that the contingency planning adopted will be realistic and effective. It is important to recognise that risk assessment and contingency planning should be conducted well before the time where resources are required or engaged. Risk assessment should always be one of the fundamental precursors to any engagement or undertaking. The failure to recognise the threats to a proposed venture is one of the key reasons why it fails. If you have all of the necessary information and have conducted all of the requisite planning for any business undertaking then proceed – otherwise do not.

Summary

Foresight is our ability to determine what may happen based upon our knowledge and experience. It is not about reading a crystal ball but about weighing up relevant factors and considering the implications. The principle behind its importance is to exercise a form of prescience that enables you to plan. We can never plan with total clarity but leadership imposes the responsibility to prepare for the eventualities of any course of action chosen. This may be based on experience or it may simply be a gut feeling. Whatever the mechanism, it is essential to any endeavour that the potential impacts, risk and consequences are assessed before commencing.

The fundamental principle in exercising foresight is to pre-empt where action *may* be required. The ability to pre-empt develops through experience and practice. To be able to appraise the current situation, recognise the strengths and weaknesses, consider contingencies that may arise, is critical to being in control.

Leadership tips

Executives:

Engage external expertise for risk assessment to ensure that it is performed objectively. Internal risk assessment is often coloured.

Project managers:

A comprehensive project plan can contain a wide array of elements but always ensure that the stakeholders have agreed on the proposed areas beforehand.

Entrepreneurs:

Cash flow problems are all too common for fledgling businesses. Identify these types of situations before they occur and have in place a strategy to deal with it. This will avoid sleepless nights, knee jerk reactions and potential failure.

Decisiveness

If you start to take Vienna – take Vienna!

N

The maxims...

Maxim XXIX

When you have the resolve to fight a battle, collect your whole force, dispense with nothing. A single battalion sometimes decides the day.

Interpretation: Attitude and resolve are indispensable when confronting any situation. When you decide to act then do so without prevarication.

Maxim VI

At the commencement of a campaign, to advance or not to advance is a matter for grave consideration, but when once the offensive has been assumed, it must be sustained to the last extremity...

Interpretation: If you decide to act then do so with determination and conviction. It is always better to take the initiative and maintain momentum than to have circumstance dictate your actions.

Maxim XCVI

A general who keeps fresh troops for the day after the battle almost always is beaten; one must employ, if useful, one's very last man, because, on the day after a complete success, there is no obstacle left...

Interpretation: Use the resources that you have when the opportunity arises. Commit with everything that you have to increase your chances of success.

Maxim XXXVIII

It is difficult to prevent an enemy, supplied with pontoons, from crossing a river... the moment the General has ascertained his inability to oppose the passage, he should take measures to arrive before the enemy, at an intermediate position between the river he defends and the place he desires to cross.

Interpretation: Take immediate steps to counteract any situation that threatens your objective or poses a risk of losing the initiative.

Napoleonic application

There was a certain indefinable quality or, as the French would say, *je ne sais quoi,* about Napoleon's ability to influence others. His conviction and self-belief inspired others to follow sometimes without fully knowing why, and sometimes without being in agreement with him. He certainly did not have the stature to lord over others, and the French were not inclined to follow blindly, so what was his secret? Some have attributed it to his will – a drive so strong that it was magnetic.

It is well known that the fundamental attributes for the success of Napoleon's campaigns were speed and decisiveness. While others prevaricated, Napoleon acted. Napoleon's self-belief and dogged determination were signal attributes supporting the apparent ease with which he directed almost any situation. When any foe dared to oppose him he always acted swiftly and without prevarication.

Story in a box – The Prussian Campaign (1806)

Following the defeat of the Austrians and Russians by the *Grande Armée* at Ulm and Austerlitz the only obstacle that stood in the way of France establishing its imprimatur over Europe was Prussia. Napoleon proposed terms, among them the co-operation of Prussia against England. These were brusquely rejected compelling Prussia and France to prepare for war.

The difference in approach taken by Napoleon and the Prussian commanders in the process leading up to the ultimate engagement is an object lesson in decision-making. On one side was Napoleon; upon hearing of the declaration of war by Prussia he immediately dispatched armies to the north and south to keep any intervention by England and Austria at bay. It was critical to not allow the Prussians to be supported by any of their allies. Napoleon placed his northern and southern armies on alert to prevent the possible involvement of any supporting force. At the same time he dispatched a large and well organised army to quickly engage with the Prussians, aiming to meet them on their own territory as quickly as possible. Several corps marched independently to converge on the Prussians forces. Every approach point was covered. The Prussians were not so much being engaged by the *Grande Armée* as being trapped by them.

On the other side were the Prussian generals; debating about which strategy to select, who should be in command, and how they would go about pulling together their outdated army. Committee's were formed. Delegations were sent out to their allies. Then they deliberated some more.

While they were debating the various issues to follow up their declaration of war the *Grande Armée* were *en route*. Napoleon's strategy and tactics were formidable. The Prussians were separated and engaged in areas of Napoleon's choosing. Even with the unexpected occurring (such as Napoleon not personally facing the main Prussian forces at Jena) the overall goal was achieved in dramatic fashion. The entire campaign was marked by speed, momentum and action. The Prussians basically never knew what hit them.

Many historians have regarded the twin battles of Jena and Auerstadt, which comprised the Prussian Campaign, as the apogee of military strategy during the Napoleonic wars. . This campaign demonstrated all of the trademark elements of Napoleon to act decisively through good planning and an overwhelming commitment to achieve the final goal.

Despite his confidence and self-belief Napoleon also possessed an amazing knack for cajoling and winning over people. Other commentators have noted that it is likely that his ability to win over others lay in his Corsican heritage. Corsicans were known to be passionate and driven yet possessing a strong sense of loyalty, honour and dignity. When Napoleon wanted something he pursued it relentlessly regardless of whether it was an object or a person.

The same passion applied to Napoleon's approach to decision-making. When a decision was required he made it without prevarication or consternation. Whether the decision was good or bad at the time was not important. Action was everything.

Contemporary relevance

Decision-making is a quality that is expected of management but decisiveness is the characteristic that distinguishes the achievers. Lee Iacocca, the man that rebuilt Chrysler from a failing auto manufacturer into a world class competitive organisation, once said: 'If I had to sum up in one word the qualities that make a good manager, I'd say that it all comes down to decisiveness...in the end you have to bring all your information together, set up a timetable, and act.' Analysis, preparation and planning are all basic requirements for making any decision but it is only action that achieves outcomes. The qualities of drive and conviction are central to leading others.

Story in a box – Donald Trump

The roller coaster ride that has been Donald Trump's career is enough to make most people shrink into oblivion. At any time during his spectacular rise his business has been in debt to the tune of billions. Having learnt the business of property investment from his father Trump started his career with the acquisition of a single high profile Manhattan property. He had never purchased any property in Manhattan before and had never developed anything but he saw the opportunity to buy the undeveloped land at a time when the New York market was in a slump. The land was developed into inner city housing and sold for a profit of $6 million. There was nothing much different about this transaction from what his father had done except for one key actor – the location.

On the back of this deal Trump decided that value conversion was the key to real estate success. He next bid for an abandoned rail yard, redeveloping it into luxury accommodation. Following on from this he then acquired property in central New York for the proposed New York convention centre. Underbidding his opposition he promised to build the centre at over $100 million less than other developers.

Then came the hotel acquisitions and a string of prestigious constructions: Trump Tower, Trump Parc, Trump Palace, Trump World Tower and Trump Park Avenue. Property acquisitions overseas followed and the Trump empire went global. A slump in the property market during the early nineties saw his business, and himself, on the brink of ruin but true to form the deal-maker extricated himself and bounced back to be on top again. Never one to shrink from a challenge he subsequently diversified into a range of other business ventures as well. In his words: 'Be bold - boldness comes from a confidence and belief in one's self... Be decisive - decisiveness comes from providing direction and being distinctive... Be energetic - energy is about passion, a fiercely competitive spirit and a bull-dog approach to winning... '

Trump's ability to roll with the punches and remain focused kept him at the top of one of the worlds toughest industries. He has always advocated buying the best properties at the best locations, quite unconventionally. His relentless pursuit of this goal has underpinned his success. Trump has always held a 'think big' attitude and not settling for second best. His brash and arrogant style seems to engender confidence even if it does not win many friends. Deal-making became an art form under Trump. To him the deal was everything. Trusting his own instincts and acting in the pursuit of his goal meant acting contrary to the advice of those around him on several occasions.

At the time of making a decision there is only decision or indecision. Decisions should be made with the resolve to follow them through. There will be times when you have total support from those around you and there will be times when it is equivocal. While it is necessary to ensure that the requisite support is in place for your decisions to be effected, a spirit of conviction is also very persuasive. This is not to say that a 'gung-ho' attitude is prescribed but once a decision is made it should be pursued with conviction.

Be ready to act

Many of us will be aware of situations where management have apparently committed to a course of action only to not proceed. The effect can be significant; people lose focus and become disillusioned. Prevarication and indecisiveness create contempt and disbelief. If, at the same time, management fail to keep people informed the situation can quickly disintegrate. Any new plan is met with doubt and cynicism. This is the domain of indecision.

It is critical to always have a plans, be prepared to act and keep subordinates informed. The absence of this can lead to people losing touch with the objective. A plan provides focus and communicates what needs to be done. It gives purpose and clarity to a course of action. Even if there is an interruption to the momentum it can be explained and managed.

Act with conviction

Action based leadership received significant attention during the 1970's as a means for motivating and encouraging people to deliver. One of its key proponents was author, academic and leadership guru John Adair. His Functional Leadership model (subsequently developed into the Action Centred Leadership Model) advocated that your actions are more important than your personal attributes in determining whether people will follow you. Adair's model of leadership demonstrated that there should be a balance between three basic components: task, team and individual. Each of these elements needs to be considered whenever a decision is made. His model advocates that it is necessary to develop both the team and the individual. While action is important in achieving the task people should be engaged on an individual level and on a team participation level. Concentrate on the achievement of the task only can lead to being perceived as having an autocratic leadership style. While no one would reject the assertion that Napoleon's management style was autocratic he recognised the importance of building a team and empowering individuals to achieve a goal. Leadership is more than just leading from the front. The role of the team and the individual should always be of equal importance. As Napoleon once said in relation to his role as Emperor: 'To attach no importance to public opinion is proof that you do not merit its suffrage'. Action is one thing but listening and engaging those around you are also important.

Summary

Decisiveness is the ability to take a position and commit to a course of action. No advantage can come from indecision. Moving people from one state to another requires someone to make decisions and be committed to the course. Prevarication and complacency are not a state in which any leader feels comfortable. If you decide to do something then do it, if not then don't – as the saying goes: 'if you think you can do something you're probably right, if you think you can't then you're right again'.

Leadership tips

Executives:

Does you organisation have a five year plan? Do you have a goal for the end of the financial year in relation to things other than profit and sales? Vision transcends the role of ensuring that the Board and Shareholders are satisfied. Staff, suppliers and the community should be considered in the development and progress of your organisation. Increase the support and value of the organisation by involving all people affected by your actions.

Project managers:

Project schedules, Gantt charts, PERT diagrams are all valuable tools but they should never be a substitute for a good plan and approach. Ensuring that the team is aware of the approach will empower them whereas following a schedule will control them. An empowered team is an effective team.

Entrepreneurs:

Once you have performed the necessary planning and preparation then act with commitment and confidence. The way you go about executing your goals is a key contributor to is successfulness.

Integrity

It is literally true that you can succeed best and quickest by helping others to succeed.

N

The maxims...

Maxim LXXI

Nothing can excuse a General taking advantage of knowledge gained in the service of his country, to fight against it, and to deliver its ramparts to foreign nations; this crime is condemned by the principles of religion, morality, and honour.

Interpretation: Your first obligation is to act in the interests of the organisation that you serve. There is no moral or ethical justification for disloyalty or betrayal.

Maxim LXVIII

There is no security for any sovereign, for any nation, or for any General, if officers are permitted to capitulate in the open field, and to lay down their arms in virtue of conditions, favourable to the contracting party, but contrary to the interest of the army at large...

Interpretation: The objectives of the team and the organisation come first. Placing your interests above your team or organisation to secure your own ends is contrary to the overall objectives of the organisation and to those whom you owe a responsibility.

Maxim LXXXVII

A General in the hands of the foe has no power to give orders; to obey them is criminal.

Interpretation: Discussing confidential matters with competitors is never appropriate. Your loyalty and fidelity is to your own organisation regardless of the circumstance.

Maxim XCIX

In war a commandant of a place is not a judge of events; he should hold till the last moment; he deserves death when he surrenders an instant sooner than he is obliged.

Interpretation: The total commitment of a person is required for any undertaking until it becomes apparent that continued resistance is futile.

Maxim CX

Conquered provinces should be kept in obedience to their conquerors by moral means... Hostages are one of the most powerful of these means, but then they should be numerous and chosen from the chief men; and inhabitants should understand that the death of the hostages would be the immediate consequence of the violation of faith.

Interpretation: Act towards others in a moral and reasonable manner. The abuse of your power will only serve to undermine it.

Napoleonic application

Napoleon is often maligned as an ambitious and unscrupulous opportunist. This view overlooks the myriad of benefits brought about as a result of his rule and initiatives. It must be remembered that the time in which he lived was characterised by warfare. Nationhood was at stake. While he profited handsomely from his military campaigns and achieved greatness of epic proportion he was ultimately reflecting the values of his country. First and foremost he was a soldier, but as a man he acted with integrity to those around him – even his enemies.

Story in a box – Code Napoléon (1811)

During Napoleon's reign significant legislation was introduced that changed the social landscape of Europe. Of significance was the French Civil Code of 1804 that commenced the process of dramatic reform. By 1811 it consisted of a body of work covering civil, commercial, penal and criminal legislation, which later become known simply as the Code Napoléon.

The introduction of a consistent set of laws for the French people was long overdue. The situation was exacerbated by the inconsistencies between the laws of other European nations. Legislation throughout Europe was a patchwork of various customs and traditions that often conflicted on some of the most basic rights. Even in France the laws in the northern part of the country differed from that of the south, for example, the north was fundamentally subject to the legacy of Teutonic law while the south, Roman law. This situation pervaded Europe and left an individual confronted with conflicting civil and human rights. To remedy this Napoleon commissioned a council to promulgate a codification of a unified French law that was simple, straightforward and 'understandable by any citizen'.

The French revolution had sparked a new sense of idealistic fervour and gave rise to the principle that the common man should be freed from the shackles of oppression by the ruling class. The rule of the monarch was to be replaced by the rule of law. While the Code Napoléon was far from perfect (most notably in relation to women's rights) it did clarify simple human rights. Unlike England which had marginalised its monarch's power through a bill of rights under the Magna Carta, the other European countries were still autocratically governed. With a hotch-potch of legislation across Europe the rights of the individual were arbitrary at best.

The French revolution had also vaunted the new Republic to become the leading light for the salvation of Europe from the tyranny and oppression of the *ancient regime*. The Code Napoléon stood as a seminal document testifying to this belief. It is debatable whether French imperialism was driven by this idealism or whether pecuniary interests were at its core, but one thing that is for certain is that Napoleon believed in equality. He advocated that every man had the right to self-determination and that talent should be the yardstick by which one is judged, not birth. This was driven out of a firm belief that the Code gave people the basic rights that they deserved. In a letter to his brother Joseph (King of Westphalia) he once said about the liberation of Germany: "What the German peoples desire with impatience, is that persons who are not of noble birth, and who have talents, shall have an equal right to your consideration and to public employment (with those who are of noble birth); that every sort of servitude and of intermediate obligations between the sovereign and the lowest class of the people should be entirely abolished. The benefits of the Code Napoléon, the publicity of legal procedure, the establishment of the jury system, will be the distinctive characteristics of your monarchy... I count more on the effect of these benefits for the extension and strengthening of your kingdom, than upon the result of the greatest victories. Your people ought to enjoy a liberty, an equality, a well-being, unknown to the German peoples... What people would wish to return to the arbitrary government of Prussia, when it has tasted the benefits of a wise and liberal administration? The peoples of Germany, France, Italy, Spain, desire equality, and demand that liberal ideas should prevail... Be a constitutional king'. Even though the French revolution had abolished the monarchy Napoleon knew that people still needed to be led. The difference was in the integrity with which they were led.

On St Helena Napoleon looked back over his life and often mused over the constant warfare during his time. Warfare would not have been necessary had Europe been a united nation. Well before the European Union existed he spoke of a united Europe that overcame the cultural differences that divided the continent. He once told his close confidants on St Helena that 'Europe thus divided into nationalities freely formed and free internally, peace between States would have become easier: the United States of Europe would have become a possibility...I wished to found a European system, a European Code of Laws, a European judiciary; there would be but one people of Europe.'

Napoleon firmly believed in his crusade to spread the ideals of the revolution to other European countries. While power ultimately became too intoxicating and derailed his moral compass, he did believe in a pan-European system, albeit under

French governance. His army carried the revolutionary ideals of fraternity, liberty and equality which had delivered freedom to France across Europe. Ultimately his belief in self-determination prevailed and underpins the democratic values and institutions that exist throughout Europe to this day.

Contemporary relevance

Integrity is largely an inherent trait and is developed in us at a very early age. To a large extent integrity is based upon our sense of right and wrong – our morality. It is derived from the people closest to us such as our parents and teachers. For most of us it is based upon the ethics of our religious or spiritual upbringing. Our morality tells us what is just and fair, good or evil and so on. How we exercise these is thus a measure of our integrity.

Story in a box - Nelson Mandella

South Africa has been both an anachronism and paradox in world affairs for most of the twentieth century. Castigated and ostracised for its ruling white government's policies the nation has gone through a tumultuous development. Originally settled by the Dutch and English in the seventeenth century, the Dutch, known as Afrikaners, established their own colonies free of English rule around the Transvaal. During the nineteenth century diamonds were discovered in the region and this led to conflict with the English and ultimately resulted in the Boer War. Greed and suspicion between the white classes became entrenched in a country that was ultimately owned by the indigenous African people.

Control of the labour market required control of the African people. To do so the Afrikaner National Party established apartheid with the aim of maintaining domination and ensuring segregation between blacks and whites. Everything from jobs to travel was controlled and enforced by a brutal police state. Native black Africans were forced to carry passbooks to be able to cross their own country. Protesting these injustices simply resulted in jail, torture and deportation.

Into this scene of injustice came the African National Congress (ANC), a party formed by several young, idealistic African men; Nelson Mandella among them. Mandella had the benefit of a legal education and possessed a keen interest in human rights. Growing up in a country where he was treated more like a foreigner imbued a deep, visceral resentment. With no other way to seek freedom and equality than to resist the unfair laws of the day the ANC instituted a Defiance Campaign during the fifties to oppose the all white government and bring the country to a stand-still. As a result Mandella was charged and confined to his home town of Johanessberg, with the removal of his 'passport' which curtailed his right to travel.

Undeterred, Mandella established a legal practice in Johannesberg and began dispensing advice to the people that had been evicted from their land, or any number of other injustices that characterised the apartheid state. A legal practice conducted by negroes for negroes quickly came to government's attention. Notice was served to relocate to a remote part of the country. This would clearly have the effect of making it inaccessible to their clients. Mandella and his partner simply stayed put and continued to practice.

The ANC movement gained momentum in direct proportion to the harassment of Mandella's practice. When his practice became too large it was simply outlawed by the government. Mandella was arrested again and the ANC movement went underground. From respected lawyer to castigated outlaw Mandella was now not even able to earn a living. With no other way to resist the injustices of the government the ANC transmogrified from a peaceful resistance organisation to a quasi-military force. Mandella and the other leaders had come to the unfortunate realisation that there was no other way than to use violence to oppose the corrupt South African regime. He was elected leader of the ANC shortly after, and began enlisting neighbouring countries' support. Returning from his crusade he was arrested and charged with travelling without a passport.

Conducting his own defence he defied the court and admonished racism. Without recognising the authority of the court he was escorted to a state prison on the following departing words: 'I have fought against white domination, and I have fought against black domination. I have cherished the ideal of a democratic and free society in which all persons live together in harmony and with equal opportunities. It is an ideal which I hope to live for and to achieve. But if needs be, it is an ideal for which I am prepared to die.' The trial resulted in him being jailed for five years. While serving this sentence he was charged with sabotage and re-sentenced to imprisonment for life.

Meanwhile his legacy grew. Acts of defiance became widespread and the world looked on in disgust at the injustice of apartheid. In desperation the ruling white party attempted to have Mandella recognise their rule by offering inducements such as releasing him in exchange for the revocation of his principles. His incarceration only steeled his resolve and the offers were simply rebuffed with the retort that prisoners have no rights to negotiate, only free men do. His taunt was to make them realise that they would need to release him unconditionally before he would enter into any negotiations.

Exasperated, and under intense international pressure, the ruling white party released Mandella in 1990. He immediately renewed his cause for equality and justice and rejoined the ANC. In 1991 a general election for President was held he was elected South Africa's president. Apartheid had been defeated. Mandella shared the Nobel Peace prize for overcoming one of the greatest blights in his country's history. To this day he is a symbol of democracy, justice and freedom.

What ought be done

In Richard De Georges 'Business ethics ', he describes morality as '... the efforts to guide one's conduct by reason – that is to do what there are the best reasons for doing – while giving equal weight to the best interests of each individual who will be affected by one's conduct'. Leadership requires that we act in a manner that is moral/ethical. Doing 'what ought be done' means that we should act in a manner where any personal or professional interests are removed and you act according to what is right. The same principles underpin justice – to act purely on the basis of the facts and the application of accepted principles.

Doing what 'ought to be done' is sometimes in opposition to the most profitable, expedient or preferable. One simple test is to consider whether your actions would be appropriate if the same situation was applied to yourself. How would you perceive the consequences if the situation were reversed? Is the organisation being regarded as more important than the individual? Is the action being taken in good faith? What are the consequences of your actions? What rights are being affected? These questions will help determine how you should act in any situation where another party's interests are affected. Integrity is acting in a manner consistent with personal beliefs and sometimes acting to your own detriment.

Ultimately, 'leaders are people who do the right thing' says Warren Bennis and Bert McNannus in their book 'Leaders: the strategies for taking charge'. Doing the right thing takes courage but is ultimately a sign of integrity. You can't please all of the people all of the time but at the very least you can do what you should and not what is expedient.

Ethical considerations

Ultimately leaders act in the interests of their organisation. A leader should also consider the impact of their organisations interest on society and the country, and increasingly on the planet. Environmental considerations are becoming even more important with greater public awareness and social conscience. A salient example is the "quadruple bottom line", which imposes the requirement for corporations to adhere to also consider ethical, environment and social considerations. Integrity is acting in a manner which demands that these responsibilities are met not just because you have to, or because it improves the image of the organisation, but because you believe in it. An ethical leader needs to have the inner belief in what they are doing is right.

Summary

Leadership imposes an obligation to ensure that words match deeds. Acting with integrity is a sign of a strong sense of morality and doing what 'ought be done'. Decision-making requires the consideration of competing priorities which often imposes upon us the obligation to act fairly and reasonably. The fundamental rationale in any ethical decision is what should be done such that all competing interests are considered. Integrity is about being true to your word and doing what is right, despite the cost to you personally. Integrity in leadership underpins the social contract that exists between you and the people that follow you. It is the basis upon which trust and respect are founded.

Leadership tips

Executives:

Have a set of values that apply to yourself and your team. Just because you have the authority may mean you can act by a different set of rules but don't expect people to willingly follow the ones that are different for them when you don't also abide by them.

Project managers:

Benefit's assessment involves a consideration of the impact of the project on stakeholders. While it is generally conducted from a financial perspective it should also include the impact on rights. These may not always be quantifiable but they can sometimes be more important than those that are.

Entrepreneurs:

Starting out with strong moral foundations is key to future success. Without it an organisation can quickly deteriorate. This must be continuously emphasised by good leadership.

Courage

L'audace, l'audace, toujours l'audace!

$\mathcal{N}$

The maxims...

Maxim LXV

...The only true wisdom in a General is determined courage.

Interpretation: Courage is the well spring of sound and effective decision-making.

Maxim XVIII

Surprised by a superior force, an ordinary General occupying a bad position would seek safety in retreat; but a good commander will put a bold face on it and march to meet the foe. By such action he disconcerts his opponent, and, if the latter shows any ir-resolution in his march, a skilful General, profiting by this moment of indecision, may even hope for victory, or at least gain the day by maneuvering; at night he can entrench himself or fall back on a better position. By such bold action he maintains the honour of war, that important essential in the strength of an army.

Interpretation: Inferior leaders retreat when the going becomes tough - superior leaders seize the challenge and act.

Maxim LXXXI

It is rare, and difficult, to possess at one time all the qualities of a great General. What is most desirable (because that draws a man out at once of the common line) is to maintain an equilibrium be-tween his mind and abilities, and his will and courage. If courage prevails more in his composition, the general will undertake de-signs, the whole possibility of the attainment of which he has not thought out; on the other hand he will not dare to carry his ideas into execution, if his will or courage is inferior to his abilities.

Interpretation: Courage provides the impetus to act. Thoughts, ideas and concepts are only as good as the will and desire to pur-sue them.

Napoleonic application

Napoleon adamantly states in several maxims that capitulation was not acceptable and that one fights until the end. Only when completely beaten does one re-
sign themselves to the inevitable. Courage should endure until the end. Respect
accrues from your attitude to persevere and continue on. We remember the acts
of people that have tried and failed more so than those that have succeeded easily. Napoleon is a salient example. There have been many commanders throughout the ages that have had amazing success. Some of them have not failed yet
Napoleon's appeal remains timeless because of his faults. On a good day he was
a Titan and on a bad day a Prometheus. But his self-belief and conviction were
always inspiring.

Story in a box - The departure from Moscow (1812)

On a clear, cool autumn day in October, 1812, Napoleon and the Grande Armée
departed Moscow. Even though there had been no substantive result in taking the
city the army's spirits were high – they were going home. Numbering around
100,000 soldiers and hangers on, the French left the burnt out city. Wagon trains
were loaded with booty and pockets were filled with the spoils of the ancient capital. The French had, after all, taken the city; they strode through the deserted
streets into the countryside. Further honour awaited the Grande Armée on their
trek westwards against the pensive Russian Army.

Then the snow came. A month later the Grande Armée was in ruin. Divisions had
been reduced to hundreds rather than thousands of men. Soldiers were dying by
the day in the bitter cold with temperatures plummeting below minus 30 degrees.
By mid November the situation was becoming desperate. The Russian army had
now adopted the practice of setting up their artillery and just shelling the retreating troops. With no hope of moving quickly through the snow the French soldiers
simply awaited their turn to be decimated.

After a long and painful trek the army finally crossed the Dnieper river into Orsha with
only the Beresina to cross into Minsk. On the verge of annihilation Napoleon took
charge of the disintegrating army; reallocating horses to the artillery, burning excess
baggage of unnecessary booty, punishing commanders that did not enforce strict discipline and taking strong steps to ensure that soldiers retained their weapons and remained with their units. But it was the action of one man in particular that galvanized
the army once again and lifted their spirits when all seemed lost – Marshall Ney.

Ney's division had been the last to leave Smolensk for Orsha. By this time the Russian army, now in hot pursuit, had effectively surrounded Ney's six thousand men.
The Russian commander, Miloradovich, offered Ney the option to surrender. The
offer was curtly rejected. Not merely because of Ney's indomitability but because
the French knew what awaited them as prisoners. Completely outnumbered, and
in anyone's estimation in a totally hopeless position, Ney attacked the Russian
army. Wave after wave of men attacked an entire Russian corps. Even General Miloradovich applauded the bravery and tenacity of the French.

When night came Ney's division had been reduced to a mere two thousand men. Although they had fought bravely it seemed obvious that the following day would not see any of them survive. Capitulation was unthinkable, so Ney ordered his troops to set camp and light fires to give the Russians the impression that they were encamped for the evening and preparing to fight the following day. Under cover of darkness, he and his remaining men slipped across the Dnieper and around the Russians. Trudging through the snow in the dark, in an unknown country, with the Russian army a stones throw away, Ney's courage gave his men hope. In the words of one of his aides '...the presence of Marshal Ney was enough to reassure us. Without knowing what he intended to do or what he was capable of doing, we knew that he would do something. His self confidence was on par with his courage. The greater the danger, the stronger his determination, and once he had made his decision we never doubted its successful outcome. Thus it was that at such a moment his face betrayed neither indecision nor anxiety; all eyes were upon him, but nobody dared to question him.'

When Ney's bedraggled division eventually rejoined the main force there was euphoria. Men that had given up under the extreme conditions found new resolve to not only continue but fight their way through the Cossacks and Russian army. Napoleon had previously dubbed Ney 'the bravest of the brave' and claimed that he would give most of his fortune to retain a man of such courage in the army. This incident reaffirmed his claim. The actions of Napoleon and Ney ultimately saved the Grande Armée from annihilation in the Russian retreat. Their leadership was all that was left in what was a completely hopeless situation.

Contemporary relevance

When you suffer a set back what is your natural reaction? If you see it as something to overcome and take control then that demonstrates resilience, which is the wellspring of courage. It is said that the things that challenge us, the set-backs, are the things that make us stronger and wiser. Challenges should not be viewed as problems but as opportunities to make us shine, grow and develop. Standing firm against adversity and meeting a challenge is an act of courage. When conditions become overwhelming then it is the leader to whom people turn. This is when true leadership is demonstrated. It is at this point that decision-makers are tested. An ordinary leader will retreat while a great leader will resist and seek to turn the tide of events. Courage is underpinned by confidence which is necessary to promote a vision for others and have the conviction to pursue the right path. We are all familiar with situations where circumstances place exceptional demands upon us. Under difficult circumstances effective leader rise up to meet the challenge and show, through courage, the fortitude to overcome adversity.

Story in a box – Martin Luther King

Born the son of a Baptist Minister in the days when the south of the United States was blemished by discrimination and prejudice. Despite the country having gone to war with itself a hundred years earlier over the issue of racial equality, Negro's were hardly better off as free men. Apartheid was the norm in the South with negro's excluded from a range of employment opportunities, banned from shopping in certain stores, not permitted to use 'whites' amenities, forced to travel in the back of the public transport and even not able to drink from certain water fountains. By anyone's standards the situation in a country with a Constitution which advocated that 'all men are born equal' was ludicrous.

During the fifties King was elected as a Pastor of the Baptist church and took responsibility for the advancement of coloured people. His first challenge was to overcome the segregation of whites and coloured's on public transport. A peaceful boycott took place and was eventually supported by the Courts banning such segregation. During this time King and his family were subjected to intense harassment and violence. Their house was bombed and racial slurs directed at them on several occasions.

Undaunted, King pushed on with a conviction and self-belief in what he was doing was right. He worked tirelessly in pursuit of a goal of equality and justice giving over 2500 speeches and travelling thousands of miles across America to deliver his message to often hostile crowds. He was assaulted numerous times, arrested more than twenty times and ridiculed, spied upon and jailed. Despite this, he galvanised a nation to see the injustice that blighted their reputation.

By the end of the fifties the civil rights movement was in full swing and gaining greater attention from the highest levels of government with President Kennedy acknowledging the fundamental principles being advocated by its followers. King never backed down in his pursuit of what was right. Despite large areas of his own country rejecting his actions the rest of the world gave tacit approval when, in 1964, he was awarded the Nobel Peace prize.

Four years later while attending a strike of garbage workers in Memphis, Tennessee he was assassinated. Gone but not forgotten the courage of Martin Luther King lives on to this very day through his actions and through his immortal words:

"I have a dream that one day all men will be judged not by the colour of their skin but by the content of their character..."

These words have echoed around the world and through generations. The vision and courage that King showed has been an inspiration to all.

Stand up for what is right

Courage in the business context is based upon the ethical belief in what is right, or what is known as moral courage. Having the conviction to pursue what should be done is also intrinsically related to integrity. It is not easy to oppose the norm and do what is right. Many organisations have faced the wrath of the public because they knew that their actions were intrinsically wrong. In many cases leaders need to make a choice between self-interest, organisational interest and third party interests. Whenever a moral question is raised between these interests then a leader will need to determine whether their decision is right and morally justifiable. Justifiability is not defensibility. The order of consideration for justifiability should be from the other party's perspective rather than your own. You may have an obligation to other parties, such as shareholders, but that should always be balances against external parties interests. Courage is then the act of doing what is right according to sound moral reasoning. A true leader will always weight up these considerations before acting.

Despite your best efforts situations may turn against you. No situation will be so bad that there is not a possibility of turning it around. Being prepared at all times and possessing the courage to oppose adversity is the marque of a competent and courageous leader.

Courage and responsibility are intimately related. When we choose to be responsible for our actions we are exercising courage. This can be difficult in any organisation where responsibility is often spread across a number of people in various positions. You can choose to sheet home the blame to someone else and save your skin or you can chose to accept that your role as a leader imposes the obligation to accept the failures of others. As we have seen, an essential attribute in leadership is integrity and this too requires you to act as a role model for the people that report to you. You need to demonstrate that your actions match your words and that you have the courage of your convictions. Demonstrating ethical behaviour is as much a responsibility as it is a mark of courage.

Be supportive
Courageous leaders are not threatened by competent people, they look for them. A weak and ineffective leader will see a competent and confident person as a threat to their position. They will seek to marginalise them and minimise the threat. Courage involves developing people and making them the best that they can be, even if they may perform better than their superiors. Strong leadership supports others and provides the means for others to succeed. The success of a team may be attributed to an individual contribution by a team member or members but it is always a function and indication of the value of leadership. Without such leadership team performance is an unknown quantity.

The business environment is becoming increasingly complex and tumultuous. Managers are required to deal with an ever increasing rate of change and stresses. Dealing with change is an important function of leadership as leaders are generally the progenitors of change. Change makes an organisation grow. Taking people from the status quo in a new direction takes courage on the part of all involved but a leader is looked to as the primary change agent. As such the leader needs to demonstrate that they believe in what the team are doing and motivate others to follow. 'Walking the talk' requires that you promote the objectives that are to be achieved and are prepared to overcome obstacles. This requires dedication, commitment and drive to succeed – attributes that are underpinned by courage.

Summary

Courage in leadership emanates from self-confidence, conviction and dedication. We generally associate things like bravery and resistance with courage but it can also be shown by the stance we take on issues and the resolve to stand by what we believe is right – moral courage. Courage is needed to make tough decisions, to take charge and be responsible, to oppose the status quo and do the right thing, to pursue a difficult course of action. In every sphere of human endeavour people will always follow someone that demonstrates that values transcend the self-interest. Courage is showing people that we mean what we say. The backbone of leadership is courage.

Leadership can be a lonely path. You are charged with responsibility and many expectations. To have what it takes means possessing attributes that stand you apart from the crowd. Courage is the quality that makes others follow and achieve results. As the quote by Robert Frost goes: 'Two roads diverged in a wood, and I took the one less travelled by, and that has made all the difference'.

Leadership tips

Executives:
Being a 'real' leader means having the courage to do what is right for all, not just the organisation and shareholders.

Project managers:
Tell it like it is. The project sponsor and business owner want to hear that the project is on track but you need to let them know the truth 'warts and all'. You manage the process – let them manage the business.

Entrepreneurs:
The odds are always against the start up. Focus peoples attention on the positive aspects and ensure that morale is maintained despite the difficulties.

Ingenuity

Impossible. N'est pas Francais?

$\mathcal{N}$

The maxims...

Maxim VIII

A General-in-chief should say to himself during the day: "If the enemy's army were to appear on my front, or on my right or on my left, what would I do?" And if he finds the question hard to answer, he is not properly posted, things are not well ordered, and he must put matters right, and at once.

Interpretation: Expect the unexpected and always have a contingency plan.

Maxim X

When an army is inferior in number, inferior in cavalry, and in artillery, it is essential to avoid a general action. The first deficiency should be supplied by rapidity of movement; the want of artillery by the nature of the manoeuvres; and the inferiority in cavalry by the choice of position...

Interpretation: Know your weaknesses and the means to overcoming them.

Maxim XL

Strong places are useful in offensive as in defensive war. They could not indeed stop the advance of an army, but they offer excellent means of delaying, checking, weakening, and harassing a victorious enemy.

Interpretation: You should make use of everything at your disposal to achieve your ends, even those things that are unconventional. Taking steps to thwart a competitor are always of value.

Napoleonic application

During the first Italian Campaign Napoleon requested one of his commanders to take the Lodi Bridge over the river Adda. The Austrians had retreated over the bridge and placed cannon along the banks. There they awaited the French. After surveying the situation the commander of the assault contingent advised Napoleon that it was *impossible* to take the bridge. 'Impossible? Napoleon replied 'is that French'? His sardonic response was typical. Not only was the bridge taken but Milan was entered days later.

This remark has also been loosely translated as 'impossible is a word found only in the dictionary of fools'. The reason why Napoleon disparaged the suggestion of something being impossible is because he always believed that there was a solution. The ability and 'genius' of leadership is finding that solution.

Story in a box – The Beresina manoeuvre

During the retreat from Russia in 1812 one of the greatest threats to the egress of the *Grande Armée* was the unseasonal melt that took place after the unseasonal blizzards. Rivers swelled and burst their banks creating a marsh of ice and debris. Crossing them became increasingly difficult for the exhausted soldiers trudging through the bitterly cold conditions. On top of this the Russian army and Cossack horsemen were in hot pursuit. The flooding was a well known phenomenon to the Russians and in order to trap the French many bridges were subsequently destroyed along the path of retreat.

In particular, the Russians had now destroyed the bridges over one of the largest rivers that the *Grande Armée* had to cross - the Beresina. Even though the French had bridging equipment they had little time with which to repair or erect a suitable bridge and shepherd across almost 100,000 people including women and children as part of the retinue of the carriage train. It was quite clear to Napoleon that all the advantage lay with his assailants. As they approached the Beresina he knew that his army was surrounded with his opponents now on both sides of the river. Their only chance of escape would be to cross where the Russian were not. The questions still loomed ominously - where and how?

In a display of characteristic ingenuity Napoleon's solution was to mislead the attackers by staging a false crossing point south of their present location. He quickly detached a force to give the Russians the impression that his army would cross downstream while at the same time dispatching another smaller clandestine force northwards to locate a suitable bridging point. The force marching south gave the impression of being the vanguard for the *Grande Armée* while the north bound force cloaked their movements and appeared merely as a detached lost unit. During this time the remnants of the *Grande Armée* prepared to meet the approaching Russian army in the middle.

Faced with overwhelming odds Napoleon's confidant Armand de Caulaincourt noted that 'the Emperor showed himself to be greater than his misfortune. Instead of discouraging him, these adversities brought out all the energy of this great character; he showed what a noble courage and a brave army can achieve against even the greatest adversity'. Still others were cynical of the escape and his most senior Marshall, Ney, stated to other officers that if Napoleon was able to extricate them from the impending predicament then 'he is the devil himself'.

While the French were in a position to cross the river at the town at Borisov Napoleon had a bridge built further north at Studzienka. As the Russians marched south the *Grande Armée* went north and secured their passage across the swelling Beresina. When the Russians realised they had been duped they quickly converged on Borisov. The *Grande Armée* had now been able to cross the bridge allowing the rear guard to establish a defensive perimeter. Rather than fighting for their survival in a trap the *Grande Armée* was able to extricate itself and inflict heavy losses on the Russian Army. Napoleon had cleverly deceived his opponent at the moment when complete Russian victory could have been obtained. The resulting 'Beresina manoeuvre' has become a copy-book tactic for evasion during a fighting retreat – perhaps one of the most difficult battle tactics.

What appeared to be a totally hopeless situation was transformed through ingenuity. Despite plummeting morale, the cold, starvation, and exhaustion the *Grande Armée* fought their way out of Russia and avoided total annihilation. While the losses of men and material in that failed campaign was nothing short of cataclysmic the *Grande Armée* were not defeated by their foe in detail and did not succumb to the Russian forces.

Several of Napoleon's maxims have been heavily influenced by the traumatic retreat from Russia. Napoleon and his commanders were called upon time and again to come up with novel approaches to dire situations. Making the best of a bad situation relies upon having confidence in ones abilities to overcome obstacles.

In this collection of maxims Napoleon indicates the quality of ingenuity by always asking how you would deal with a new situation if it was to emerge suddenly and what steps would you take to overcome it. This approach emanates from a constant analysis of what is going on around us. Asking yourself 'what if' type questions constantly will mean that you are always considering the potential implications that may adversely affect any undertaking. This action is a necessary and essential precursor to the exercising of ingenuity. You have to be on your toes to move quickly - being ready is to be prepared.

Contemporary relevance

The root of the word 'ingenuity' is closely related to 'genius' and is indicative of the ability of the superior mind to solve problems. This does not imply that leadership means having all the answers but bringing together the expertise of everything at your disposal and facilitating the solution when individuals themselves may not be able to see it.

Ingenuity is the ability to see solutions to problems while others are still focussed on the problem itself. Leadership involves thinking outside the square, not being bound by the status quo, and seeing opportunity in any situation - even in adversity.

Story in a box – Steve Jobs

Steve Jobs and close friend Steve Wozniak started Apple Computer company in their home garage with the Apple I in 1979. Five years later they released the Macintosh (Mac) with its innovative white screen, real text display and drop down menu system that were accessible with a remote control device known simply as a 'mouse'. The Mac was revolutionary at the time for its user oriented features and minimal design.

By the mid 1980's the battle-lines had been drawn between the Mac on one side and the IBM PC on the other. People were fanatically parochial. The Macintosh was seen as inventive, clever and technically superior to the dull text based PC. The PC still dominated the market because it was cheap and open to a multitude of software systems while the Mac remained proprietary.

Just when Apple was on a roll the wheels fell off. The new CEO wanted to compete head to head with the PC market and proposed the heretical possibility of an 'open' architecture that others could copy so as to replicate the same success that IBM had in making their architecture an industry standard. Jobs left Apple in 1984 at the critical point in the ascendancy of micro-computers. A decade later Apple were reporting annual *losses* in excess of $1 billion dollars. The product range lost direction with a series of ill conceived concepts. Apple was on the ropes and almost out of business by the end of the nineties.

The board of Apple called on Jobs to return and rescue the failing company. After some cajoling and intense negotiation he accepted the role of CEO and quickly introduced an entirely new look for Apple with the 'iMac' range. Widely regarded as the funkiest looking computer on the market it captured peoples attention and imagination. Everything about it was different. Yet it still had the feel of a 'Mac'. Hot on the heels of the iMac came the iPod with Jobs sensing that the portability of digital information was about to explode. He was right on target, again, and the iPod became one of the hottest consumer accessories in history. It became the 'must have' gadget at the turn of the century. This was followed by the iPhone, iPad and a raft of ingenious computer products. Apple subsequently became the largest and most successful computer manufacturer on the planet.

The driving force behind the success was Steve Jobs primarily because of a "no compromise" attitude on the ingenuity and creativity of the business.

Ingenuity is not just about using creativity but also about using any of your attributes to provide a competitive advantage. If you are a small organisation operating in a market dominated by large competitors then your advantage is your ability to move quickly and adapt to any market disruption. Reorganising and re-engineering a large firm takes time, so focusing on the work that your larger competitors are unable to perform provides a market advantage. Seeing the gap in the market is as important as being aware of how to address the means to tap into that market.

More often than not great leaders are formed under the pressure of great adversity because they take a different approach and are able to free people from conventional thinking. During the second word war the feeling that gripped Europe as the Nazi war machine decimated all opposition led to despair in England. Many English citizens began preparing for invasion and fled their homes (while at the same time wondering where they would go on their small island location). But one man posed an alternative view and focussed the nation on what they could achieve and identified their inherent strengths. With four simple words Winston Churchill galvanised the spirit of a distraught people: 'We will never surrender".

Self-reliance

It might be thought that ingenuity is an inherent trait. People are either creative or not, they either see things differently or not. This may be true but there are still other fundamental attributes of the characteristic that need to exist and that can be developed, such as resourcefulness and self-reliance. Resourcefulness is about identifying the means for success in any situation. Self-reliance is about looking into yourself and having the confidence to rely upon your own beliefs and ideas. Exercising ingenuity is about being able to see the opportunities when they may not be apparent and using your own 'smarts'. It takes practice to develop, but it can be improved through the development of core abilities and skills like self-reliance, resilience and resourcefulness. There are many ways this can be done – take up a new hobby or sport, do something challenging, write a book, give a presentation, start a club, take up public speaking etc

Ask what if?

So what are the tools and techniques that might be used to exercise ingenuity? As seen under the section on foresight, many of the same techniques used to spark ingenuity are also relevant: simulation analysis, sensitivity testing, risk analysis and so on. These techniques basically focus on asking the 'what if' question. Simulation analysis (sometimes called scenario analysis) relies upon looking at a range of possible events that may impact the scenario that has been selected. For example, we might decide to pursue a certain property acquisition. In doing so we would consider the implications of various interest rates and investigate the movement of property prices. The different rates of interest on the borrowed capital provide various scenarios to be considered. These scenarios or 'simulations' help us to decide on the most appropriate course of action such as the most likely property price fluctuations, rates of return and acquisition strategies. Similarly, sensitivity analysis looks at the impact that a particular variable might have on an outcome to determine the impact relative to changes in the input variables. Both techniques are based on the fundamental principle of risk assessment – what is the impact and likelihood of an event occurring. The obvious result of any form of risk analysis is to determine how to mitigate the consequences of the event. It is at this point that we need to exercise ingenuity and analyse the things that might happen. There is no guide book for finding solutions to unexpected events. Ingenuity is about reaching into our experience and drawing on our intuition to come up with a solution.

Most of the time risk analysis is nothing more than common sense. But common-sense, as they say, is not so common. This is where being 'street-wise' and having good political nous comes to the fore. Napoleon had this quality – he knew the nature of man. People with this ability are able to read the undercurrents and instinctively know what is going on. There is no magic to it as most of the time it is based upon having the competence in your area of expertise and the empathy to understand the agenda of others. Napoleon's maxims on studying the past and learning what we can about our environment are critical to developing these abilities. What may appear as common-sense is really an ability to see things as they should be seen, and having the confidence of those around you so that they see things your way. Competence and empathy provide us with the core qualities to be able to propose creative solutions. It becomes natural, at least to the people that have developed these qualities, because they see the environment differently.

Business planning is all about trying to determine what we need to achieve and how we go about applying the resources we need. Resource considerations impose an obligation to determine what might go wrong. Whatever form of analysis is conducted the end result should always be to have some form of contingency plan in place. While structured assessment of possible contingencies may prepare us for the unexpected there may arise situations which defy such planning. It may not always be possible to avoid these situations but when they occur your creativeness will be called upon. Leadership is about demonstrating that a solution exists and motivating others to over come doubt.

Summary

Within the ambit of ingenuity are a range of qualities: resourcefulness, initiative, self-reliance, creativity, resilience, preparedness. Ingenuity enables you to act proactively and decisively, providing direction to people so that a solution emerges. Leadership provides the means to promote an open and collegiate environment to explore new ways, promote new ideas and foster creativity. At the same time leadership can be demonstrated through the proposal of a creative solution as a result of your own inner 'genius'. Having the courage to propose your ideas and following them through acts as an inspiration for others to follow.

Leadership means focusing on the solution and not the problem. Ingenuity is the ability to take problems and issues and see a solution rather than an obstacle. Careful analysis of the current situation is necessary so that the full range of options are explored. It is essential that a leader takes action when a problem arises.

Once you have decided upon a course of action then move quickly and decisively. Decisions made on instinct cannot wait around to be analysed. If you are going to develop your ability to be creative in decision-making then you must pursue the course of action with confidence.

Leadership tips

Executives:
Don't just consider SWOT when exploring a strategy but PESTEL as well, especially in these days of the quadruple bottom line.[5] This technique possesses several other key components that should be in your mind.

Project managers:
You will not make many friends trying to persuade the project sponsors that the project cannot be completed on time or within budget at the beginning of the project. Inform them of the likelihood and consequences, record their response and proceed. It is better to have a compelling case based on evidence than a hunch at the beginning of the project.

Entrepreneurs:
Pursuing your dreams is daunting. Remember to keep things in perspective. Executing an excellent idea badly is worse than executing a bad idea well. Make sure that you call upon the right expertise when you need it to execute your ideas with the best possible chance of success.

---

[5] SWOT analysis is basically a strategic planning tool used to evaluate the Strengths, Weaknesses, Opportunities, and Threats of any undertaking while PESTEL analysis is mainly concerned with the environment surrounding a venture or organisation at the macro level. It considers the Political, Economic, Socio-cultural, Technological, Environmental and Legal consequences of the undertaking, project or venture. SWOT forces us to ask questions about what effect will certain external factors have on the undertaking while PESTEL looks at how the undertaking/organisation will impact on certain external attributes.

Indefatigability

When defeat comes, accept it as a signal that your plans are not sound, rebuild those plans, and set sail once more towards your coveted goal.

N

The maxims...

Maxim XXIII

*When you are occupying a position which the enemy threatens to surround, collect all your force immediately, and menace **him** with an offensive movement.*

Interpretation: When confronted with a difficult situation act boldly and decisively to overcome it. Acting with audacity and confidence will build your confidence and demoralise your opposition.

Maxim LXVII

...In an extraordinary position, extraordinary resolution is needed; the more important the resistance of any body, the better are its chances of being succoured or of cutting its way through. How many things which appeared impossible, have been done by resolute men...

Interpretation: Meet every situation with the resolve to succeed. The greater the challenge the more ardent should be your approach. Any situation can be turned around with the right attitude.

Maxim XXVII

When one is driven from a first position, it is well to rally one's columns sufficiently to the rear to prevent the enemy interposing, for nothing could be more untoward for columns to be attacked separately before their junction.

Interpretation: If you do not succeed at first then take steps to ensure that you do not fail on the next attempt. Maintain unity at all times.

Maxim LXXXIII

A commander-in-chief never gives rest either to the victor or to the conquered.

Interpretation: Leadership transcends success or failure and continues on until the job is done.

An army can pass always and in every season wherever there is room for two men's feel.

Interpretation: Nothing should stand in your way where there is the possibility of success and the will to achieve it.

Maxim XVIII

Surprised by a superior force, an ordinary General occupying a bad position would seek safety in retreat; but a good commander will put a bold face on it and march to meet the foe.

Interpretation: Maintain composure and focus even in situations where you may not be in control. Do not be dissuaded by your situation – resolve and attitude counts for more.

Napoleonic application
Story in a box – Escape from Elba

In 1813 the *Grande Armée* met the allied powers of Europe at Leipzig. What was to become known as the 'Battle of the Nations' was also to end in the defeat of the French with Paris capitulating and Napoleon being forced to abdicate. Napoleon faced a combined Russian, Austrian, Bavarian, Prussian and Swedish force that had all but surrounded the city of Leipzig where the *Grande Armee* had chosen to make its last stand. The battle was one of the most sanguinary of the Napoleonic period. The French took terrible losses during the fighting withdrawal but still managed to avoid total annihilation. While the city of Leipzig was eventually taken by the allied powers, the French had resisted a monumental assault with valour.

As the European nations closed in on Paris Napoleon refused to capitulate. A series of battles to save Paris ensued. Marching westwards the *Grande Armee* fought on the retreat. Completely outnumbered by the combined force and with some of his allies capitulating, Napoleon and his marshals fought on. This was not blind courage but defiance that almost paid off. At the battle of Hanau the French almost turned the allied attack into withdrawal. The battle to take Paris continued for half a year, contrary to the belief that the end came after Leipzig. The final battle in the Paris campaign at Arcis-sur-Aube in 1814 saw Napoleon and his marshals at their best. Optimistically, Napoleon strategised to defeat his opponents once and for all. He showed all the signs of his former self, capable of dealing with any eventuality.

The battle at Arcis-sur-aube had only just commenced when a shell exploded right next to Napoleon. His horse fell and threw Napoleon onto the ground with shrapnel tearing his mount open. His aides looked on in total shock at the cloud of dust and then hurried to Napoleon's aid. Now 45 years of age Napoleon hopped up without effect and demanded another horse. Dumbfounded, his aides stood silent as he rode away to direct battle operations elsewhere.

Despite the continuing operations around Aube the allied forces had by now marched into Paris on another front. Despite the ongoing resistance the war was lost. The two marshals defending the city were faced with signing an armistice or having the city destroyed. The following month Napoleon was forced to abdicate.

With the *Grande Armée* beaten the allied powers subsequently resolved to imprison Napoleon on the isle of Elba. This small isle, off the coast of Italy, was to be patrolled by the English Navy to prevent any chance of Napoleon escaping. After his abdication he was transported by ship to the isle that was to be his final home.

Elba was not much of a location with only a small community of basically agrarian peasants. Napoleon's residence was modest but he immediately set about commissioning works to improve it. Rather than see the isle as a prison he began running it as his principality. A number of projects to invigorate the isle ensued: vineyards, new roads, new school – even a military academy! Almost every facet of the peasants lives was covered by some new decree or initiative.

But Napoleon grew restless, he could not accept defeat and wanted to return to France to continue his destiny (and partially redress the injustice of his exile). Planning commenced for his escape a mere six months after his arrival on Elba. On 26 February 1815 he evaded the English patrols to slip ashore onto the mainland. Arriving with just over a thousand men he then proceeded to return to Paris.

In his absence the Bourbon monarchy had been restored. When the King heard of Napoleon's arrival on the coast of France he was livid. Marshall Ney was despatched to bring Napoleon back to Paris 'in an iron cage'. In what has become legend, Napoleon and his men engaged with Ney's forces just south of Grenoble at La Mure. Wanting to avoid a conflict for fear of its possible ramifications throughout France, Napoleon walked towards the front lines of troops that had taken up aim; opening his coat in dramatic fashion, he beseeched the soldiers with the following words:

'Here I am. Kill your Emperor if you wish. The forty five best heads of government in Paris have called me from Elba and my return is supported by the three first powers of Europe.'

While Napoleon's claims were apocryphal they had the desired effect; rather than a fusillade Napoleon was met with cheers of *Vive L'Empreur*. He returned to Paris not with the thousand men with whom he had left Elba but escorted by more than 10,000 soldiers which led to the rapid collusion of the rest of the army. He took up residence as Emperor once more and began to seek terms with the allies. When this failed he prepared, once again, for war.

Contemporary relevance

Indefatigability is a leadership trait that motivates and inspires. A 'never say die' attitude is indispensable in situations of high pressure, competition and in times of crisis but it should always be tempered by sound judgement and a focus on the ultimate goal. Leaders need to be able to demonstrate the dual qualities of composure and laser focus under pressure.

Story in a box – Rupert Murdoch

The man behind one of the worlds most dominant and influential corporations has worked tirelessly to achieve his vision. Born in Australia and growing up with a father that owned a local newspaper business, the *Adelaide News,* Murdoch had a comfortable career ready and waiting for him. Sent to Oxford University to receive a first class education it was apparent from the start that his life would be marked by privilege. Yet despite the opportunities that lay before him Murdoch took his first job at the *London Daily Express* to learn the ropes of the highly competitive newspaper industry and understand the intricacies of the family's business in a different country that would prove instrumental to his future. Returning to Australia at age 23 he took up a position in the *Adelaide News* and quickly became conversant with all aspects of his fathers newspaper. Several years later, in the early fifties, he took over from his father and then went about purchasing other local newspapers that were losing money. These he quickly turned around, demonstrating a knack for reinvigorating failing businesses.

At 28 he purchased his first television station in Australia (*Channel 9* Adelaide). This was followed by the acquisition of his first interstate newspaper (the *Mirror*) and the establishment of a national newspaper (the *Australian)* in the face of entrenched competition from the newspapers of the day. His Australian business interests flourished. By this time, well into his thirties he was worth in excess of $50 million. He was certainly in an enviable financial position and able to retire quite comfortably. Instead he pressed on.

The opportunity presented itself to acquire a share of the London based business *News of the World*. This opportunity allowed Murdoch to move into foreign media . A short time later he acquired *The Sun* with its broad working class readership. The paper was transformed completely, despite stiff resistance from management and Unions, and allowed Murdoch to introduce innovations that revolutionised the business. Circulation of *The Sun* increased seven-fold as a result of the new tabloid format and other changes.

On the back of this successful foray into the UK market, four years later Murdoch acquired a stake in the US newspaper the *New York Post*. He then acquired a string of smaller papers and eventually built up a strong US base. He later acquired the *Times* in London and the *Sun-Times* in the US city of Chicago. By the mid eighties News Corporation was now worth several billion US dollars and owned over eighty newspapers in several countries.Most people would simply stop at that point and be content with a very successful global media organisation. Not Murdoch. The new technologies that were to mark the end of the twentieth century saw a spate of high profile acquisitions that catapulted News Corporation to the position of being the largest media conglomerate in the world.

Murdoch now decided to begin acquiring a greater stake in other media with Twentieth Century Fox being acquired in 1985. To move into television he then acquired the Metromedia Company, changing his nationality to that of US citizen to circumvent their foreign media laws. In the UK he broke the Unions grip on the newspaper industry by relocating the printing press operations from London to Scotland; fighting an acrimonious campaign to overcome entrenched Union control.

Murdoch then set about entering the satellite television market. He had failed twice to do so with both Fox in the US and Sky in the UK costing him tens of millions of dollars. Despite the risks and losses, and with mounting debts and bankers baying for repayment of huge loans, Murdoch took the bold step of acquiring the Asian *Star Television* network. This not only gave him a television network in the growing Asian region but allowed News Corporation to extend its reach into the massive Asian market. The networks coverage crossed borders from the Middle East to Japan requiring a morass of different legislation to be negotiated with different governments. This, in itself, would have been a lifetime effort to resolve the issues involved yet was taken on with the usual aplomb.

Throughout the nineties Murdoch continued to consolidate his existing base and extend his control of the lucrative television market. A string of sporting team acquisitions followed with an ever increasing control of sports broadcasting. By the new millennium he owned several of the worlds largest sporting clubs, including Manchester United, and now had a controlling interest in DirectTV, acquired for the sum of almost $7 billion, giving him the single largest satellite television network in the US. An industry official noted at the time that '... he understood the power and reach of satellite television and has been indefatigable in pursuing that vision. He had been trying since the mid-80s to get into the satellite television business in the United States and had the door slammed in his face three or four times before the DirecTV deal. You have to credit him for having a vision to see how satellites can be used for one particular, very powerful, application.'

News Corporation was now the largest media empire in the world with several hundred businesses across the globe and revenues in the tens of billions. His personal net worth was also in the billions. At the age seventy he has indicated a determination to keep on going. His often ruthless and uncompromising style has seen him create as many enemies as friends but his continuous pursuit of the impossible seems to drive the people in his employ to do the same, with them often citing his energy and enthusiasm as infectiously motivating. What motivates him is the turning of failure into success, taking risks, and overcoming obstacles. With a Promethean nature of being able to achieve the impossible and overcoming cataclysmic situations with his persuasiveness, Murdoch's persistence and determination has transformed a modest Australian newspaper into the world's largest media empire.

It has been widely acknowledged that the only certainty today is change. Dealing with change is something that every organisation must face to survive and grow. It is uncomfortable for many people but inevitable in organisations if they are to adapt to succeed over their competitors. If the business is not meeting customer expectations then it must change and understand what change is required.

Focus

It is critical to any significant change initiative to ensure that the outcomes, the strategic direction, and the strategy pursued by the organisation are aligned. Being on the lookout for threats and having contingency plans to counter them is essential. Contingency planning is an important consideration where any change agenda involves significant risk. This might be as simple as considering a strategy to address the consequence of inadequate resource allocation through to adopting an approach to counteracting a potential take-over. Indefatigability is not simply fighting on against all odds but being prepared to meet any contingency with a definite purpose and plan and remaining focussed on achieving the outcome.

Every business will face opposition, not only from competitors but industry organisations and even the government. Leadership is marked by the ability to withstand the pressure, stay focussed and push on. There is no more inspiring act than a person faced with overwhelming odds and finding the way through. Of course this requires courage but the act of navigating through a difficult situation and remaining focussed on the goal is an elemental nature of indefatigability.

Discretion

While indefatigability and courage may be admirable they may also manifest themselves in obsessiveness. Many famous battles have been fought to the death with the courage and spirit of the vanquished lauded throughout history – Thermopylae, Constantinople, Zama, Alamo, Gallipoli, Stalingrad, to name a few. While the gallantry of the warriors has become legend, fighting to the death is obviously pointless where an alternative exists. Living to fight another day is a key message in several of Napoleon's maxims even though this would seemingly contradict his edict of never capitulating. However, there is a clear distinction between refusing to give in and risking complete defeat. You should always know when you are beaten and take steps to ensure that the loss is as least costly as possible, or learn from the defeat to come back even stronger. If possible this means that you should seek to avoid a complete loss through steps to thwart your opponent and stall for time to resume under better circumstances. It is far better to obtain a marginal victory than risk a pyrrhic one, just as it is far better to accept a defeat and have the resources in place to resume at a later date.

Summary

Indefatigability is the inspirational force of action based leadership. Whether it is in the form of tenacity, indomitability or fortitude the possession of this quality is necessary to succeed. The leaders that possess this characteristic have vast reserves of inner strength and a firm belief in both themselves and the goal they pursue. This also serves to motivate and encourage others. Often bordering on obsessive behaviour these leaders demonstrate persistence in the face of failure and determination to overcome obstacles that others would simply not be prepared to face. This quality inspires others to believe and give their best. Setbacks and disappointment are taken in stride. People stay committed and focussed on achieving the goal.

As the aphorism goes 'when the going gets tough, the tough get going'; indefatigability is the ability to rise up and face challenges. Having a vision and imparting it to others is essential to true leadership but following it through is often where the greatest challenges are to be encountered. Leadership is about inspiration. The people that we respect are often the people we want to follow. No one wants to follow someone that quits in the face of tough obstacles. We also don't want to follow people that blindly pursue things that are pointless and excessively risky. There is therefore a fine line between being a maverick and being shrewd. So while this quality may be a necessary leadership attribute there are other attributes that are needed to temper it: judgement, integrity, competence and responsibility. Like anything in life, it is a matter of balance.

Leadership tips

Executives:

It is far better to manoeuvre around opponents to achieve your objective than to confront them head-on. Engaging in organisational politics and personal power-plays may be professionally, even personally, rewarding but if this does not contribute to the overall objective then it should be avoided.

Project managers:

Sometimes following the process and doing everything by the book will not achieve the desired goal. Project managers have to oscillate between being people managers, financial controllers, technical experts, task drivers and so on. Flexibility in performing the role will often achieve a more beneficial outcome.

Entrepreneurs:

Every fledgling business starts out with a goal. Over time this growth can often move in directions that do not support the overall goal. It is important to always be aware of how any new diversification or acquisition supports the overall goal.

Leadership action

This section will look at the manner in which Napoleon was able to achieve his goals, that is, identify what capabilities he considered important for success. From this we can obtain a picture of how a leader of Napoleon's calibre achieved his vision. For instance, it is clear from several maxims that Napoleon placed high importance on planning. This was a core skill which he regularly employed. He saw it as his responsibility to create the strategy and not something that could be devolved to others. This is not to say that he did all the planning but the overall strategy was his domain. His vision and the strategy to support it were indivisible.

Many observers have considered his approach to leadership, in the contemporary context, as 'hands on'. He was not simply a visionary but a man of action. No detail was too insignificant to escape his attention. He did not simply watch from the sidelines – he was an active participant. He led in the field and always took personal charge for everything that went on. Leadership, to him, was not about delivering speeches and holding the highest office, it was about being seen to do the things that were necessary, and having the courage and responsibility to pursue them. These qualities were also evident in his generals, inspired by the desire to imitate the success of his leadership.

Strategy and tactics receive a fair amount of attention in his military maxims. His prescriptions ranged from high level factors, such as the use of the corps system, speed and concentration of force, through to the elements at the personal level, such as motivation and communication. No detail was too small to escape his attention, even the manner in which troops were to cover terrain:

Maxim III

An army which undertakes the conquest of a country has its two wings either resting upon neutral territories, or upon great natural obstacles, such as rivers or chains of mountains. It happens in some cases that only one wing is so supported, and in the others that both are exposed. In the first instance cited, namely where both wings are protected, a general has only to guard against being penetrated in front. In the second, where one wing only is supported, he should rest upon the supported wing. In the third, where both wings are exposed, he should depend upon a central formation, and never allow the different corps under his command to depart from this...

We can see that inherent in the directions is an overall understanding of the environment and the capability of one's resources. Napoleon's strategy derived from an acute awareness of the capabilities at his disposal. This was an essential prerequisite for his planning – the fundamental requirement of any military strategy. In business this is equally important for, as they say, failing to plan is tantamount to planning to fail.

It is important at this point to clarify what is meant by strategy. What do we mean when we say that we have a strategy? How do we prepare a strategy? It is interesting to note that the word 'strategy' only entered the English language in 1810 in response to scholar's attempts to come to terms with Napoleon's approach to warfare. In much the same way as 'infrastructure' has today become ubiquitous for the resources of an organisation (not its original intent), strategy too has fractured into differing concepts. Napoleon's military strategy was predominantly based upon the attribute of it being a plan, with a strong emphasis on using deception to gain an advantage. His strategy was innovative at the time even though it largely drew on the techniques of previous great captains. It also rarely changed from the principles that he employed in each of his campaigns. This has often been a reason why he was ultimately able to be defeated.

For our purposes strategy is simply the implementation of a stratagem, which, by definition, is a scheme, device or trick for obtaining an advantage. Whatever the approach the aim is to achieve an end result. Leading author and management strategist Henry Mintzberg describes strategy as including: plan, ploy, pattern, position or perspective. Strategy as a plan infers that it is developed consciously and purposefully, as a ploy it is intended to outwit an opponent, as a pattern it may 'form' and become something that was not intended, as a position it could be the location that you wish to occupy, and finally as a perspective it can be a perception of what you are or wish to become. This gives strategy a multi-dimensional and organic quality. It could be your overall plan or it could be the development of a particular method of operating.

Of all the attributes of strategy Napoleon was a great proponent of situational strategy. The success of his campaigns were due, to a large degree, to the attention that he paid to all aspects of the planning process. This is increasingly the case in the modern business environment with the application of project management techniques becoming commonplace. Planning should be central to any organisations activities. The reality is that more often than not it is more likely that an initiative is commence and then the planning follows. For Napoleon there was always the purpose and then the plan.

Napoleon's view of strategy was embodied in the famous quote: 'strategy is the art of making use of time and space. I am less concerned about the latter than the former. Space we can recover, time never'. Strategy was about employing what you had in the most effective manner to achieve an outcome in the least amount of time. Only through consummate planning could this be achieved. One of the best known commentators of the day, Karl Von Clauswitz, in his seminal work during the Napoleonic Wars, 'On War', noted from a lengthy observation of Napoleon's campaigns that 'strategy is the use of the engagement for the purpose of the war. The strategist must therefore define an aim for the entire operational side of the war that will be in accordance with its purpose. ... The aim will determine the series of actions intended to achieve it.' Establishing a purpose and then pursuing it with a plan of action is fundamental. In other words ask 'why am I doing this?' and 'how will it be done?'

Story in a box – The Continental System

The Napoleonic period was not simply a case of 'total war' because of one mans desire for power. While it is true to say that without Napoleon the *Grande Armée* may not have been as pugnacious the fact remains that the political situation in Europe at the time was very complex and the need to be on a war footing was central to a country's survival. In an age where expansionism was the norm there was both a very real threat from foreign invasion and at the same time the opportunity for a country to obtain a significant commercial advantage. The rivalry between nation States was not only caught up in the fight for survival but the desire for prosperity.

The European nations had been at war with each other for decades, if not centuries. As with most conflicts the driver was essentially for resources – land, people, raw materials. France believed in the concept of its 'natural frontiers' which consisted of all land from the Rhine river in the East to the Pyrenees in the West and the Alps in the South. Austria also had designs on the northern parts of Italy around the Alps. Prussia laid claim to the Rhine land. England needed the northern countries above France to remain neutral to act as a buffer to French aggression. In this environment the movement of France to secure its natural frontiers made it inevitable that the European nations would be in perpetual conflict.

The French revolution certainly did not make matters any better. The English were ardently Royalist and saw the beheading of the French monarch as barbaric. The other continental monarchies saw the deposing of a monarch as an existential threat to their regime. An uneasy détente existed post 1789 between France and the other nations with internal politics taking precedent over foreign affairs.

All this changed when the ruling body of France commissioned Napoleon to invade Italy, which necessitated the involvement of Austria. Following the defeat of the Austrians came the new threat of invasion of England. Considering the success and reputation that had accompanied Napoleon's victory over Italy the threat of invasion was perceived as imminent, and with good reason, as Ireland threw in their lot with the French. The very name of Napoleon was dreaded throughout England. The Irish support of the French in the insurgency made the possibility of invasion closer than the shores of Calais. While the invasion of England ultimately never took place it left a palpable uneasiness of French intentions.

This fear heightened when Napoleon effectively took control of the country as First Consul in 1799. Eager to smooth relations between the countries and usher in a golden age for France Napoleon sought to appease the English in his early days of power. The English saw this as nothing but a ruse. Despite Paris being the height of fashion and a magnet for English high society around the turn of the nineteenth century the political climate remained tense. Napoleon continued to make overtures to King George III in order to negotiate a suitable peace between France and England. Despite this he was snubbed in whatever effort he made - the King would not respond directly and the English government would not even concede to address Napoleon as Emperor. Relations remained indifferent. In the meantime the English actively agitated among the other continental nations to form a new coalition to overthrow Napoleon. Overtures were made to fund armies in Austria, Prussia and Russia to march against France. Assassination plots were connived and French interests throughout the continent were deliberately marginalised. The English monarchy saw France as their worst nightmare: a liberal society led by a man of common birth.

The English wanted nothing to do with the peaceful aspirations of the French and made overt their plans to restore the natural order. In response Napoleon issued the Berlin decree (1806) and followed it with the Milan decree (1807) which basically barred any English ship from entering any European port. In response England embargoed all French trade. Napoleon's aim was to blockade England so as to bring it to its knees and force her to come into the fold of a pan European community and seek an accord with France. The strategy that Napoleon employed to cow England was known as the Continental System. The underlying principle was simple: close all continental ports to English trade and effectively isolate the island, forcing them to submit. As France effectively controlled all major ports along the European coast from Portugal to Germany the plan had merit. After all, England was a trading nation and depended upon trade with the continent. Without it she would be plunged into financial ruin.

In order to evade the System the English simply traded through Russia. In 1807, Russia signed the Tilsit agreement and the System henceforth extended to Russia. This was catastrophic for England. At first the strategy had the desired effect. England was faced with a stark choice – to invade the continent and defeat Napoleon or collapse. The first expeditionary force under Wellington's command entered Portugal the same year. As a result Napoleon now had to face the English on a western front.

The Continental System drove the armies of France to every corner of Europe. As a strategy it succeeded in damaging trade with England – for both sides. France's allies were forced into the system through the submission of conquest and even France herself suffered from the deprivations. Was Napoleon simply an ambitious warmonger or an individual driven by grand vision? Many will assert the former but the reality is that his pursuit of a strategy to isolate England was a reaction to her actions against France. Regardless of the justification Napoleon had a clear strategy to bring about a pan-European community, but for English implacability.

Napoleon took what he had and used it to its best advantage through an understanding of the resources at his disposal. The same principle can be applied in the modern business environment. Professor M.E Porter, formerly of the Harvard Business School, in 'Operational effectiveness is not strategy', advocates that leadership should be primarily focused on where the organisation needs to go and how well it fits that goal. Leadership is about developing, communicating and refining an organisation's strategy so that it has a better fit with the market that it operates in or intends on operating in. At the same time the organisation needs to be steered in a direction that gives it a competitive advantage, not merely associated with greater efficiency. Strategy is about doing things differently or doing the same things in a different way. An organisational leader certainly needs to ensure that the organisation is functioning as effectively as possible, but should mainly be focussed on the bigger picture such as whether the organisation has the attributes to take advantage of new opportunities. An organisation's leaders have a primary role to move the organisation in a new direction. Napoleon encapsulates this in the following operational maxim with its dual focus:

Maxim LVI

A good General, a well organised system, good instruction, and severe discipline, aided by effective establishments, will always make good troops, independently of the cause for which they fight, at the same time, a love of country, a spirit of enthusiasm, and a sense of national honour, will operate upon young soldiers with advantage.

Strategy also provides us with the path to achieve the vision of leadership. Any vision requires a level of detail so that it can be followed and it is at this point that planning and preparation become the next most important leadership functions. Any endeavour must have a purpose or objective. Leadership provides that purpose by being able to distil the most important attribute to be pursued. Good leadership provides focus and enables people to be clear on what they are aiming to achieve. Purpose and planning are the practical manifestation of organisational strategy.

The implementation of strategy is dependant upon the capabilites and readiness of the organisation. It is one thing to have a plan but another to have the means to execute it. Napoleon did not just propose grand plans and hope for the best. He ensured that he would succeed by making sure that the elements that underpinned his campaigns were present. Artillery was a major factor in his battle plans. He knew that this was a strategic resource that would pave the way for the rest of his operations. He also knew that it was essential to be able to minimise the effect of his opponents and mask the deficiencies inherent in the French infantry. At the same time he leveraged off its capability by employing it in new and more effective ways. The introduction of a new style of military operations with the corps system also facilitated more effective operation. The old system was replaced with a meritocratic regime that inspired all soldiers that they could achieve whatever success they desired.

Leadership needs to also be delivered on a regular and personal basis. Napoleon was a great believer in maintaining contact with both his officers and his soldiers. Communications was vitally important in any operation where separated corps acted independently. Leaders need to be involved and be seen to be involved in the process of communicating and motivating the people they lead. Nothing is ever achieved by a group of people unless it is communicated. Communication in any organisation is a critical consideration to maintaining morale. The ability to capture people's imagination and have them commit to your vision is ultimately what leadership should achieve.

The action of leadership covered in the remainder of this section will therefore cover these attributes in greater detail. In summary these are:

> Purpose
> Planning
> Readiness
> Capability
> Communication
> Motivation
> Alignment

Alignment is left until last as it is ultimately the synthesis of the others. We will see that the maxims place great emphasis on co-ordination and alignment. For most of Napoleon's career this was one aspect which enabled him to achieve victory time and again until, of course, Waterloo. Even the lessons from that campaign are relevant to anyone that wishes to avoid failure, especially from hubris. We will cover this aspect and bring together all of the other aspects in the final analysis.

Purpose

Order marches with weighty and measured strides;
disorder is always in a hurry.

N

The maxims...

Maxim V

All war should be methodical, for every war should have an aim,
and be constructed in accordance with the principles and rules of
art. It should be carried on with means proportional to the obsta-
cles which can be foreseen.

Interpretation: Every undertaking should have a clear objective.
Use only the resources necessary to achieve the objective.

Maxim XII

An army ought only to have one line of operation. This should be pre-
served with care, and never abandoned but in the last extremity.

Interpretation: Any organisation should have a primary focus for its
activities. This focus should be maintained and managed carefully.

Maxim XXI

When an army carries with it a battering train, or large convoys
of sick and wounded, it cannot march by too short a line upon its
depots.

Interpretation: When hampered by constraints or an obstacle
that impedes the delivery of your primary objective then move
quickly to resolve them.

Maxim XCII

In battle, as in a siege, art is shown in directing fire from many
quarters on one point; when the fight is once begun, a leader skil-
ful enough to bring to bear on one such point, unknown to the
foe, an expected mass of artillery, is sure to carry the day.

Interpretation: Focus on the objective and pursue that with all your
efforts. Bring as much pressure to bear on the weakness of your opponent as you can. This factor alone is enough to bring success.

Napoleonic application

In war Napoleon always focussed on the primary objective – to destroy the enemy. The objective in the field was clear but there was still an underlying purpose to the achievement of that objective, which we have described as strategy. Quoting Karl Von Clausewitz from 'On War': 'strategy…maps out the plan…it affixes the series of acts that lead to [the objective]'. Napoleonic strategy emanated from several purposeful aims, be it the subjugation of England, nationalism, revolutionary idealism or expansion. Every Frenchman had a grand vision following the French Revolution which was effectively carried across Europe through the army. The *ancient regime* had been replaced and the French saw the spread of the revolutionary ideals as a duty. It was their duty to the suppressed people of Europe to restore justice and liberty to humanity. Whether Napoleon actually believed in this is another matter, but he held the same principles as he was aware that it was the revolution which had made his rise a possibility after all. Ultimately the desire to bring a new world order meant that every European nation needed to be in agreement and Napoleon set about to ensure that there was agreement; even if each nation had to be made to see the light.

Story in a box – Lisbon to Moscow

By 1807 France controlled most of mainland Europe. The Continental system was beginning to take its toll and England was feeling its effects. Despite this there was one major leakage from the continent with England – through Russia. In order to evade the System English ships simply sailed for the Baltic states. Trade boomed along this area of the coast. Napoleon entreated Czar Alexander of Russia to join the System, but to no avail. It became clear than there was only going to be one way of enforcing a total embargo against English shipping – military force.

The Czar had expressed no desire to support France in her designs to hobble England. It suited Russia to be the trading focus of Europe. To Napoleon, Russia being the new commercial focus and suborning the Continental System could not remain, and so, upon this justification the *Grande Armée* set forth toward Prussia. The Prussian army offered little resistance after their defeat at Jena/Auerstadt and effectively allowed Napoleon to march through Poland and into Russia. When the Czar learnt of Napoleon's incursion into Prussian held Poland things became a little more precarious. The Polish people had desired their own nation separate from both Prussia and Russia. This was anathema to both countries. Napoleon had to be repelled, and so the Russians set forth to meet them at Eylau. In what was one of the most brutal conflicts of the Napoleonic era, with 30,000 men left dead, the Battle of Eylau ended in stalemate. With the onset of winter both sides licked their wounds and prepared to fight on once the weather permitted. Several months latter the contest resumed at the Battle of Friedland. This time the Russian army was decimated. Napoleon was now free to march into Russian territory and do as he pleased with Poland.

Even though the Russian army could have regrouped and drawn on its vast reserves the Czar hesitated. Napoleon sent out feelers to gauge the possibility of peace. He also knew that the Austrians and Prussians could be provoked by Russia to rise up against his army so opted for a mutually beneficial arrangement. As it transpired the Czar despised the English as much as Napoleon. In a show of deft statesmanship by Napoleon the Treaty of Tilsit was signed in 1807 whereby the Russians would join the Continental System and embargo English ships. With the coastline of Europe now under French dominated control England would have a tough time holding out much longer.

Or so Napoleon thought. With the Baltic coast now inaccessible to English ships they simply went to Portugal. In the meantime Napoleon had installed Joseph, his brother, as King of Spain. Unable to control the Spanish and Portugese it became necessary for the *Grande Armée* to invade Spain, thus precipitating the Peninsular War of 1808-1812. More and more troops were absorbed into the Iberian peninsular to stem the resistance of the guerrilla attacks and the appearance of the English army at Lisbon. The war became progressively more intractable, drawing in men and material from a nation already overstretched with garrison outposts throughout mainland Europe.

With growing unrest under French rule the Peninsula war was observed with interest by the suppressed eastern European nations. English infiltration on the Iberian Peninsula became more successful towards 1810 with a growing feeling that French occupation would soon be overthrown. In 1811 relations with Czar Alexander also took a turn for the worse. Trade was re-opened with England. Once again Napoleon was forced to march against Russia. This time with disastrous consequences. Unable to stem the trade leakages through Spain and Russia the System was no longer tenable. Apart from this the countries forced to be party to it suffered as much as the intended victim. With the destruction of the *Grande Armée* after the retreat from Moscow more and more ports threw their doors open to trade with England. When French dominion faltered it was only a matter of time before old alliances became rekindled and the tide turned against France.

To a great extent the conflict between France and the other European nations during the period of 1806-1812 was driven by the strategy of enforcing the Continental System. Even though the French controlled the countries and the ports there were numerous blockade runners that were willing to take the risk and trade with England. This brought about even more stringent reprisals and sanctions, which in turn only served to alienate the conquered countries. When Portugal bucked the System France was forced to send armies to enforce it. The final straw came when Russia subsequently chose to defy France and allow open trade with England in 1812. Napoleon was forced to march against them as well. A war on two fronts drained France and ultimately destroyed her.

Contemporary relevance

What defines the purpose of an organisation? Contrary to what we may think organisational purpose is often not as clear in the business environment as we might expect. The difficulty lies in the paradox of the definition being dependant upon the audience. An employee's idea of an organisation's purpose may be quite different to the customers, or the shareholders, or investors. This conundrum means that purpose can be several things while at the same time not being any one thing.

Purpose defines what the organisation is about. Put simply, it defines the organisation. Purpose is a also a strategy. Leadership establishes the purpose and determines how the organisation will achieve it in the market. Leaders need to be sure that the purpose they propose is consistent at all levels and that there are no misconceptions, either internally or externally. Essentially if an organisation cannot answer the question 'what defines us?' then it cannot know what it is. If is does not know what it is then is cannot be sure where it will go or whether it will succeed.

Story in a box – Hewlett-Packard

In the highly competitive IT industry there is one rags to riches story that defines an organisation's dogged adherence to their stated purpose. HP became one of the largest information technology firm in the world with revenues greater than its nearest hardware rival (IBM) and miles ahead of the nearest software rival (Microsoft), yet both of these giants are often more likely to receive the press and be recognised as industry leaders.

As with many IT start-up firms HP began its existence in a home garage in 1934. The mission of Bill Hewlett and Dave Packard was to create a firm that developed innovative electronics solutions for a modern age. In the words of Dave Packard, the organisation loftily wanted '...to make a technical contributions for the advancement and welfare of humanity'. Sure it was about producing hardware that made money and addressed a market gap but underpinning that was a need to make something that was worthwhile and useful. HP had a vision and underlined it with quality.

Initially making electronics components the team quickly moved into electronic measurement equipment during the forties and fifties. The advent of the semiconductor saw HP create some of the most sophisticated mathematical computers available during the sixties and seventies. Initially described as 'calculators' these devices had more computing power, and were more effective, than the desktop computers produced a decade later. In the seventies and eighties HP became known for their printers and scanners, with these products, once again, quickly establishing a reputation for reliability and innovation. It is also not widely known that HP's foray into desktop computers predated most of the commonly acknowledged progenitors.

By the turn of the millennium HP was so entrenched in the IT market that they merged with one of their direct competitors – Compaq. The merger was the largest in history and resulted in HP going to the top of the hardware manufacturing tree.

Having a clear objective and pursuing it was not simply a pipe dream either. The company's founders were at the forefront of management techniques of the day and embodied the principles of 'management by objective'. The company also set the trend for many other firms to follow with an open corporate and communications culture, management involvement at the production level and embracing the attitude of a company supporting its staff in more ways than just financial.

The pursuit of innovative, useful and reliable equipment has resulted in HP being recognised world wide as a manufacturer of quality products. It was the reason for starting out, the reason for its advancement, and ultimately the reason why it has persisted.

Who's responsible?

Without putting too fine a point on it, determining an organisation's purpose is a leadership responsibility. Whether this is defined by the project manager for a project or chief executive for a corporation all eyes are on the leader to focus people on the objective. In a 1999 survey conducted by two US Universities of 1450 senior executives spanning 12 international organisations, the ability to 'articulate a tangible vision, values and strategy' for an organisation was seen as the most important skill for corporate leaders[6]. If the leader is not clear then neither can the people being led. An organisation's purpose must be understood by all and must emanate from the organisation, but it first needs to be formulated and promulgated by the people that run the organisation.

Examples abound of where there is a fundamental mismatch between internal and external organisational purpose. A government department that collects revenue but see's itself as a law enforcement agency cannot have a clear strategy for how it will deliver simply because its purpose is unclear. A salient example might be a Customs agency that focuses the attention of its staff on the search and seizure of drugs and policing activities rather than the taxing of imported goods. The Government's expectation from the organisation is for revenue rather than convictions. Is the organisations purpose clear? To whom? Similarly, an organisation that produces a product that is used for something other than what it is intended cannot hope to have a credible marketing strategy. For example, a company may produce paint brushes with a highly resilient bristle, marketing them as a re-usable, superior to the competition and with greater longevity. There is nothing wrong with that. However, if customers use the brush, primarily, to clean engine parts and other industrial applications then there is clearly a mismatch between

---

[6] RD Duanne & MA Hitt 'Achieving and maintaining strategic competitiveness in the 21st century: The role of strategic leadership' Beylor University & Texas A&M University

the reason for producing the product and its intended market. If the company decides to soften the bristles and make it more 'user friendly' by producing it with a soft grip and in a range of fashion colours the end result may be that the product will not meet the expectations of its target market. As a result, if the use of the product is not understood by the organisation then whatever its strategy it will not be a success. The quintessential aspect is to ensure that there is alignment between the organisations purpose and that of its stakeholders.

Setting the purpose of an organisation is a top down function. Ensuring that employees are aware of, and committed to a strategy means that they understand the objective and are aware of what is needed to achieve it. Without it an organisation simply fractures into fiefdoms and becomes progressively more difficult to control.

Organisational purpose is the fundamental driver for organisational direction. In his seminal book 'The Practice of Management' organisational theorist Peter Drucker advocated that customer focus should be at the core of business success and that the purpose of an organisation is not the profit motive but the customer need. This gave birth to the principle of 'management by objective'. While profit is essential for any business to continue to attract investment and remain viable, Drucker advocated that this will naturally follow where the focus is on customer satisfaction. Leaders need to be aware of the organisations real purpose and ensure that it is kept foremost in the mind of the people that they lead. The principle of management by objective, while dated, is still as relevant today as it ever was.

Outcome realisation

Organisational purpose is one part of the equation. The other part is the expected outcome that needs to be realised. Both of these elements are equally important. While the terms may seem synonymous there is a fundamental difference: objective is what we are trying to achieve, outcome is the resultant benefit that we will obtain. Both can be measured but the outcome is often more difficult to quantify. Objectives are generally aspirational and so often becomes the focus of people's attention: 50% market control, leading manufacturer in the sector, Number 1 service provider etc. Outcomes are unfortunately not as clear cut in most people mind: greater customer satisfaction, increased productivity, improved security. Despite outcomes often being difficult to measure it is always important to ask whether the objective supports the outcome, which may not always be a one to one relationship.

Our ability to quantify and assess the achievement of objectives is fundamental to achieving the desired outcome. A classic case was the introduction of the Dyson vacuum cleaner. James Dyson's 'cyclonic' vacuum cleaner was introduced to a market that was dominated by entrenched brands and well established technology. His objective was clear – to make a vacuum cleaner that never lost suction.

That indeed sounds appealing, but what is the resultant benefit? Greater efficiency perhaps, but would the resultant benefits of saving time and reducing effort be apparent to the consumer? Even though the Dyson vacuum cleaner was revolutionary it was marketed solely on one attribute – its objective. Clarity of objective was instrumental to the products development and its success. While it could have been marketed with a string of technological reasons for its superiority or benefits to the consumer it was simply the objective that carried it through.

Maintaining Focus

Deviating from a chosen strategy only serves to undermine people's confidence and dilute their focus. Adherence to the selected strategy is paramount in maintaining focus and commitment. There will always be obstacles that affect the ability of any organisation to maintain its strategy but these should still be met with the resolve to follow the selected course. In the business context obstacles, commonly known as risks, can often be assessed well before they may occur. The key is to move quickly to address these so that they do not distract our efforts or derail our objective.

Project managers typically consider constraints as potential obstacles. The general constraints on a project are time, cost, scope and quality are assessed during the planning process to determine what impact they might have on being able to achieve the desired outcome (for example, a certain budget may not be sufficient to achieve an expected outcome). An understanding of these will determine what approach is adopted and the impact on other constraints. Being aware of these things and assessing how a particular situation may impact a project is probably the core skill of a project manager. And for good reason, without the money the project will fail, without adequate time the project cannot hope to deliver and without a clear appreciation of the scope or the required quality then the output will not meet expectation.

Summary

Every organisation must have a strategy and every strategy must have a purpose. Purpose involves the establishment of clear objectives. Maintaining the commitment and focus on the purpose is the art of management. Establishing it is the responsibility of leadership. We may propose a 'vision' of what we wish to achieve but it still needs to be in terms that others can understand and relate. A vision needs to have a clear path to achieving it and this is established through realistic and attainable objectives.

Leadership tip

Always ensure that the objectives of the undertakings that you are managing are consistent with the outcomes. Objectives should always be precise and this is often assisted by ensuring that they are SMART (Specific, Measurable, Achievable, Realistic and Time bound). A quick analysis of any business objective against this acronym will usually reveal whether the objectives are in fact well defined. Outcomes on the other hand can be thought of in terms of benefits (and disbenefits) and should be assessed by using success criteria and performance indicators to determine whether they have been met.

Planning

It is not genius where reveals to me suddenly and secretly what I should do in circumstances unexpected by others; it is thought and preparation.

N

The maxims...

Maxim LXXXIV

An irresolute General who acts without principles or plan, although at the head of an army superior in number to that of the foe, often proves inferior in the battle field. Shuffling, half-measures, lose everything in war.

Interpretation: Without principles and a plan you stand little chance of success. Despite the advantage from sufficient resources a leader without a strategy is immediately at a disadvantage.

Maxim XXIV

Never lose sight of this maxim, that you should establish your cantonments at the most distant and best protected point from the enemy, especially where a surprise is possible. By this means you will have time to unite all your forces before he can attack you.

Interpretation: Be prepared well before the event and avoid any situation that could compromise your position or strategy.

Maxim XXXVI

When the enemy's army is covered by a river, upon which he holds several têtes de pont, do not attack in front. This would divide your force and expose you to be turned. Approach the river in echelon of columns, in such manner that the leading column shall be the only one that the enemy can attack, without offering you his flank. In the meantime let your light troops occupy the bank, and when you have decided the passage, rush upon it and fling across your bridge. Observe that the point of passage should be always at a distance from the leading echelon, in order to deceive the enemy.

Interpretation: When confronted with a major impediment exists then do not approach the problem head on but proceed with a well devised strategy that provides you with the greatest opportunity for success and denies your opponent of as much as possible to counter. A well executed and clever plan will overcome the most difficult situations.

Maxim XXXIII

It is contrary to the usages of war to let one's parks and heavier pieces of artillery enter a defile if the other end is not held also; in case of retreat they will be in the way and be lost. They should be left ready, and under a suitable escort until mastery is obtained of the outlet.

Interpretation: Even when a conflict situation appears benign prudence is advisable. It pays to be circumspect even in routine situations. Be sure to have an exit strategy that is comprehesive.

Maxim XXX

Nothing is more rash and contrary to the principles of war than to make a flank march before an army in position, especially when this army occupies heights, below which it is necessary to defile.

Interpretation: If the surrounding circumstances pose a high risk of failure then take steps to ensure that you have done as much as possible to protect against that possibility. Do not allow an opponent to obtain an advantage simply due to your own neglect.

Maxim CVI

Flank marches are to be avoided, and when made should be as short and in as brief a time as possible.

Interpretation: Don't change things when there is a sound plan and well reasoned execution in progress. Altering the execution of your strategy on the fly is foolish when it is not consistent with the initial plan.

Maxim XII

An army ought only to have one line of operation. This should be preserved with care, and never abandoned but in the last extremity.

Interpretation: Strategy should be monitored and adhered as long as it remains justifiable. It should only be changed with care and skill.

Maxim CI

Defensive war does not exclude attack, just as offensive war does not exclude defence, although its aim is to force the frontier and invade the enemy's country.

Interpretation: A proactive strategy should not exclude reactive aspects. Regardless of the overall strategy always be sure to consider the implications of the unexpected and allow for it.

Napoleonic application

Napoleon's preparation for campaigns were comprehensive to say the least. Whether it was traversing desert, crossing the sea, scaling mountains or trudging through snow the extent of the undertakings required significant planning and preparation. This was not just limited to the manpower requirements. Administrative undertakings were also significant. In the absence of real time communication systems the most significant factor in the embarkation on any campaign was to ensure that commanders and troops were well prepared and clear on the objective. Troop movement and co-ordination was paramount. Overall strategy was supported by plans or each corps Contingency plans were also in place to cope with emerging situations. Comprehensive planning was crucial.

In the maxims that deal with planning Napoleon identifies that prudence and forethought are fundamental aspects of planning. It is not necessary to have complex plans and sophisticated processes to achieve success. Napoleon's best plans were often a balance between creativity and common-sense.

Story in a box – The offensive defence

At various times throughout history military strategy has alternated between the adoption of either a predominantly offensive or defensive nature in direct consequence of the technology and tactics of the time. Early forms of warfare around the age of the Egyptians and the Greeks adopted an offensive posture. Armies basically confronted one another in the open field and engaged. Engagements were basically decided by the skill and weight of each force. During the Roman period this approach to warfare changed as greater firepower emerged. Armed fortifications and better armour were subsequently introduced to deal with the superior tactics and heavy artillery of the Roman legions. Engagements generally commenced with a barrage of projectiles followed by a well organised movement of troops under cover of large shields (known as scutum). Warfare became predominantly defensive in nature with each side relying upon fortifications and armour protection before launching any attack.

The middle ages saw a continuation of the defensive but more in terms of fixed fortifications. The advancement in artillery in the form of catapults (ballista) saw the need for more effective defences. This came in the form of castles and fortresses. These fortifications began diminishing after the middle ages mainly through the advent of more effective artillery capable of breaching their walls. Armour, which peaked with the use of full metal suits, also became redundant following the advent of gunpowder as it was incapable of protecting the wearer from small canon and musket shot. Its use acted more as an inhibitor, making the wearer slower and less agile, in other words, a better target.

Fixed fortifications and armour continued to decline in use and the offensive strategy reappeared. This trend continued into the modern age with the increasing use of technology able to overcome a strong defensive position. The Napoleonic period was marked by the use of the offensive. Defensive formations and tactics had to be completely rethought. The use of the corps system, greater firepower from canon and horse artillery all contributed to a rethinking of the way that armies engaged. In response to this Napoleon employed the 'offensive defence'.

While Napoleon has become notorious for always seeking the offensive he did so on the basis of a 'well reasoned defence'.[7] This meant that his army was always prepared to attack yet at the same time were in a sound defensive position. Assuming a defensive posture did not mean being on the defensive but being prepared to meet a superior force with an effective defensive position. The technique was refined to the point of becoming an innovation in itself.

On numerous occasions the *Grande Armée* engaged with enemy forces much greater in size and defeated them. Even though success in overcoming the opponent was the primary goal there was always a defensive alternative. The well reasoned defence acted as the fall back position. An attack was more than a *levee en mass* (mass movement) as troops attacked in a well planned assault that allowed the possibility of going on the defensive to contain and isolate the foe. It was the use of the offensive defence that often stymied opponents when they went on the counter attack. The *Grande Armée* seemed impenetrable as their offensive constituted a layered defence as well; able to withstand the enemy's assault. This was only possible through astute and well devised prior planning and preparation.

Contemporary relevance

Planning is often not given the attention it deserves in business. It is all too often simply regarded as a box ticking exercise. Documentation is created to simply meet the need of compliance and probity. Most of the time organisations are pressured to just 'get on with it'. The problems occur when things start to go

---

[7] Chess players will be familiar with this principle. Movements are made on the basis of maintaining a good defensive position while still manoeuvring into an offensive position. The art is to ensure that you have a solid defensive position to move from while still moving towards the goal of defeating your opponent. Sooner or later you need to attack but it is futile if your efforts leave gaping holes in your defences.

wrong. Why did the product fail to reach the target audience? How did we exceed the budget? Why do we not have enough people to do the work? If these things have not been considered before-hand during planning then things can come to a grinding halt. Planning is the act of pre-emption. Without it we are sailing into the unknown.

It is the leaders responsibility to ensure that planning is done properly. This does not mean simply overseeing the planning but taking an active role to ensure that it will meet objectives, support business strategy and achieve beneficial outcomes. Effective leadership means being committed to the planning process and seeing that what is produced serves the overall purpose or objective to be achieved, and that it delivers the required outcomes. Any plan or strategy requires commitment and belief in it by both stakeholders and the delivery team. It must also be able to withstand scrutiny at the time it is proposed and during its execution. This can only be achieved when diligence and involvement is exercised throughout the planning process.

National Aeronautics and Space Administration (NASA)

Think of an organisation where planning is crucial to the overall success of its undertakings and NASA would have to be at or near the top of the list. Whether it is the design of a new technology or the long range planning for a mission to the outer reaches of the solar system NASA has been confronted with some of humanities most difficult endeavours.

Formally established in 1958 out of the former National Advisory Committee for Aeronautics to pursue the development of space-science research, NASA quickly learnt to take on projects of daunting magnitude. In 1961 its scope was expanded with the Goddard Space flight centre coming under its control. Along with this came a mandate by the Government to conduct the first manned flight outside of the earth's atmosphere. In 1962 this was upped to placing a man on the moon before the end of the decade. For an organisation to be formed out of an aeronautics organisation to now have the charter to go to the moon seemed absurd when the public were still of the view that space travel was pure science fiction.

Undaunted about its new role NASA management had in fact been on the front foot a year earlier with a ten year plan that not only proposed the feasibility of manned space flight but a number of 'futuristic' ventures such as the launching of satellites to monitor the earths weather, a manned flight to the Moon, probes to Mars and Venus, and vehicles that could carry equipment into the earths orbit. In the years that followed science fiction became science fact. Sceptics of old had been replaced by believers in the possibility of achieving anything where the will and the technology existed.

To this day NASA supports their strategic planning with a range of subsidiary planning to direct their operations. While the formative and overarching plan is contained in the strategic plan (which identifies NASA's '...vision, mission, goals, and objectives') this is developed in more detailed subsidiary plans. An Enterprise plan supports the overarching strategy to 'give direction to the work of all NASA organizations and employees.' The Enterprise plan breaks down the NASA Strategic plan '...with detailed objectives, implementation strategies, and brief descriptions of their principal programs and/or processes'.

Any organisation knows that managing their finances is critical and this is no less the case at NASA with the capital investment plan essential to operations '...because the size, scope, time horizon, and technical nature of these investments are critical to long-term Agency viability.' The final part of the overall strategic planning process is the formation of the functional leadership plan '...to implement the Agency's Strategic Plan, improve Agency management, and respond to new external direction.' Each plan feeds into the other with a cyclical process of review and re-evaluation. Conducted every three years the planning process is described as 'continuous'. All of this occurs before any vehicle is constructed, astronaut trained or contract sought.

The scale of the programs at NASA are among some of the largest and most sophisticated human undertakings: the Apollo program alone expended a staggering $25 billion by 1972.[8] Today NASA has plans that extend out to 30 years to cover the exploration of the entire solar system. With human lives and huge sums of money at stake nothing is left to chance, as chance sometimes has the tragic consequence of rearing its head anyway. Regardless of whether the strategic plans posed by NASA seem like fiction the organisation is prepared to meet the unknown.

Flexibility

One of the great problems with a long term plan is that it can become something of a behemoth. As a result changing it becomes taboo and the organisation is locked in to something that may become outdated or irrelevant. One way around this is to plan in stages. Planning in stages allows work to be managed in subsets. In this way definable 'chunk' of work can be delivered before proceeding to further stages. Planning does not simply stop once a stage plan has been created. It may be necessary to formulate subsidiary plans for numerous, otherwise rudimentary occurrences. Breaking a large plan down into manageable bodies of work allows the complexity to be reduced. This technique also serves as a mechanism for review, and so allows us to determine whether the overall is on target. At the completion of a stage the strategy can be evaluated, reviewed and realigned if necessary. It also allows for the containment of risk to each stage of the execution. This can sometimes be an important consideration when each stage of the strategy is evaluated in isolation. What may appear as generic risks to the overall

---

[8] By comparison, in the same year, the Olympic Games in Munich cost $611 million to run. Today the Games are more likely to cost over $12 billion which would equate the Apollo program to roughly half a trillion US dollars in today's terms.

strategy may become quite different when a specific stage is evaluated. Breaking down a strategy may reveal quite different risks and greater uncertainty when analysed separately.

One of the fundamental principles of planning is to be prepared as early as possible. Too often this advice is ignored and the situations disintegrate into throwing more people at the problem or engaging more expensive expertise. Many infrastructure and technology projects are beset by this problem. Inadequate planning is performed and when it becomes clear what is actually required resources are brought on in increasing numbers. Rather than improving the situation it becomes worse as the new people take time to come up to speed while those aware of what needs to be done are diverted into training and familiarising the new team. Costs increase and schedules delayed. In most cases the reason why this occurs is simply because the basic requirements for the project were not understood – whether customers requirements or project requirements. In other cases it is because fundamental preparation activities are not conducted, such as the failure to determine whether the undertaking is feasible in the first place or what impact the project might have on the organisation or target stakeholders, such as a feasibility study or environmental impact study. Simply put – don't do something that is critical to the organisation without adequate preparation.

Planning should be a fluid exercise – never static. Planning should not be something that is done once and then filed (like a contract). Changing a plan should be seen as a natural consequence of changing events and circumstances. While a sound plan is the basis for pursuing any strategy the simple fact is that nothing is ever static and that change is inevitable. Changing plans to suit changing circumstances is axiomatic. This may seem obvious but too often plans are created and then cast in stone. Documents created and 'finalised' so that they cannot be touched. Any schedule created at the commencement of a project is seen as the ultimate statement of the future. We even use the term 'baselining' as a statement that the plan is locked in as if the planners had incredible prescience at the outset.

Even though significant effort is expended in the planning phase there should nonetheless be an acceptance of change in any plan. The degree of change depends upon the circumstances. The simple rule of good planning is flexibility and pragmatism. As Napoleon once cynically stated, 'unhappy the General who comes onto the field of battle with a system'; always be prepared to be flexible and adapt to circumstance. No document or plan should ever be considered the final version unless there is absolute certainty about the future - of course there never is.

Adherence

While flexibility is essential in the planning process there still needs to be adherence to the proposed strategy. If a particular plan has received approval then it should be followed if it supports the strategy. This is not as trite as it may sound. Circumstances always arise where stakeholders in any venture begin to propose various scenarios that may require changing the plan - 'what if we did this in parallel to that to save some time?' 'what if we do this later so that we can deliver earlier?' Alternate scenarios will always be promoted to gain efficiency but they should only be entertained after careful consideration. If the new reasoning is valid then the first question that you would ask is: why was it not part of the original planning process?

One of the most difficult dilemmas for a leader to face is maintaining alignment between strategy and plans. On the one hand there needs to be flexibility to adapt to changing circumstances and on the other the need to adhere to the plan. The maxims indicate the importance of following the 'line of operations' and that this should only be changed with care and skill. Simple and germane advice which is, more often than not, ignored. Strategy should never be so restrictive that it impedes creativity but it should, nonetheless, be maintained when it is selected. The art is being able to manage these competing requirements hence the need for prudence and circumspection in the changing it. It is far better to make incremental change to strategy than to decide that it is unsuitable or that planning is unsupportive. While the 'pen is mightier than the sword' the 'pencil is mightier than the pen'.

Complexity

Planning requires creativity and common-sense to reduce complexity. A plan need not be complex, and sometimes the best plans are quite simple. A salient example of this can be found in the naval warfare of the Napoleonic period. The French and Spanish navies of the day could not match the rate of fire of the Royal Navy who were better trained and more accurate. Naval battles of the time generally consisted of lining up alongside an opposing fleet and then unleashing broadsides at each other. The Navy that fired the most effective cannonades generally won. The problem for the English was that they could rarely come close enough to effectively engage with the French. French gunners were known to aim for the opponents rigging and then move out of range. This 'hit and run' tactic basically consisted of destroying the rigging and then sailing away or striking the disabled ship from long range. This posed a frustrating problem for English naval commanders in that they were never able to effectively beat their foe in detail.

Admiral Lord Nelson had a simple plan. He instructed his commanders to 'sail straight at them'. Although seemingly obvious it was however a revolutionary naval tactic of its day and prevented the opposing navies from escaping the English fleet. It also enabled the significant advantage that the Royal Navy gunners had over their adversaries. The tactic of sailing straight at an opposing fleet meant that the Royal Navy only became a large target at very close range and once through the line of the opposing fleet was able to turn onto the opposite side of the enemy ship and deliver a devastating volley. Nelson used this tactic to great effect in several engagements, but of course, at Trafalgar it spelt the end of the French and Spanish fleets opposing English domination of the high seas. It also paradoxically meant the end for Napoleon with the English able to land troops on any part of the continent unopposed. Keeping it simple makes preparation and execution far easier to achieve.

Change

Organisational change is increasingly becoming the topic of attention for many business in these days of increasing business pressures. Planning for change means engaging the necessary resources to achieve it. Changing an organisation requires significant planning whether it be to change the culture, business direction or simply to introduce a new management structure. Implementing change as a means of 'shaking things up' can do more harm than good if it is simply management's intention to keep staff 'on their toes'. This practice was *de rigueur* in many of the high tech firms at the turn of the millennium. Although the practice was not responsible for their decline it did not help either. Implementing change is a serious undertaking and requires skill and planning - not gimmicks.

All too often plans are overlooked because things appear to be going well. However, this often results in a lapse of discipline because the focus of the people involved and the objectives become vague unless reinforced and monitored. Less focus on the project (as a consequence of its seamless delivery inevitably leads to budgets being reduced or staff diverted to other activities or timeframes revised. This situation may even invite failure. The principle here is that unless you are involved in the formation of the plan or strategy then you should not intervene in its execution. If events occur during the plan's execution then the course of action that should be followed to alter the proposed plan will necessarily involve a careful analysis of the required change against the existing plan and a resultant proposal to meet the new requirements. The abandonment of the plan invalidates the very purpose of having it in the first place. If the plan must be changed then the risk inherent in doing so should be recognised and accepted by the person ultimately responsible for its implementation. External intervention in planning not only risks failing to achieve the desired outcome but undermines the confidence and motivation of the people involved.

Summary

There is one statistics upon which all are agreed in relation to the failure of any implementation of strategy - inadequate preparation. The process of planning and preparation involves investigating the fundamentals and ensuring that they are sound. Anyone who has gone down this path knows that it is the things that you neglect that often come back to haunt you. If you are told that it is not necessary to perform certain planning activities because there is insufficient time then the best advice is to ignore what you are told. Planning is essential for success; failing to plan is a prerequisite for failure.

Leadership tip

Whatever your field have a plan of action. This does not just set down the details of what you intend on doing but provides a discipline to make sure that all the necessary components are in place. Keep the plan up to date and assess achievements against what was planned to keep track of progress. Depending upon your level in the organisation will determine whether your focus is on the opportunities and achievements or the risks and the issues. Apply the principles of planning across the organisation so that everything feeds into the overall strategy in a co-ordinated manner.

Readiness

Never interrupt your enemy when he is making a mistake.

N

The maxims...

Maxim VII

An army should always, night and day, and in any hour, be prepared to offer all the resistance of which it is capable; and this demands that the troops should constantly have with them their arms and ammunition, the infantry with its artillery, cavalry and generals; that the different divisions of the army should be constantly in a position to support, sustain, and protect one another; that whether in camp, on the march, or at the halt, the troops should be always in a position of vantage, which has the qualities necessary for every battle-field...

Interpretation: An organisation should be ready at all times for any contingency. Regardless of the whether the situation seems benign or not your strategic resources need to be able to respond to any situation.

Maxim XXVIII

A detachment must not be made on the eve of battle, for in the night the situation may change - either by movements of the enemy towards retreat, or by the arrival of large reinforcements which allow it even to take the offensive and render the premature dispositions made, futile.

Interpretation: Do not alter the commitment of resources once a strategy has been decided upon. Keep the resources that you need for the task required.

Maxim CIII

Field fortifications are always of use, never hurtful, when they are well understood.

Interpretation: It is never unwise to take advantage of a defensive asset as long as you are completely familiar with them.

Napoleonic application

One of the defining aspects of Napoleon's leadership was the attention given to every level of the army. He would often conduct spot checks in the camp to be sure that all of the soldiers were ready - day or night. Soldiers were not assumed to have the correct equipment – it was checked. Field inspections were typical. Effective leadership required attending to details no matter how minor.

Even though Napoleon himself wouldn't have the time or the capacity to follow up every soldier in the army he ensured that people in his command paid attention to the smallest detail. He also knew every part of the army and its capability and ensured that dispositions were made that supported the other parts of the army so that the force, as a whole, became indomitable. Soldiers were given greater ability to live off the land, officers were given greater authority to lead, and the army as a unit provided with the armaments to be as effective as it could possibly be. From rifle effectiveness to new technology in artillery – nothing was overlooked.

Story in a box – Artillery v Infantry

French military capability in the late 18th century was hardly leading edge. The Charleville musket used by French infantrymen was approaching over twenty years old by the turn of the century. Inaccurate and unreliable; it was not able to effectively hit anything over 250 metres and was prone to fouling and misfiring. On top of this the French infantrymen were not great marksmen as they were poorly trained and often conscripted into the army from the peasantry hoping just to be fed. Artillery was not a great deal better with outdated cannon and field operations. This all changed following the French Revolution under Napoleon. To remedy the deficiencies in the infantry Napoleon placed greater emphasis on the practice of using bayonet advances, following a devastating cannonade, that diminished the resolve of the opposing army and decimated their structure. This achieved greater shock and awe than the more traditional practice of lines of troops firing volleys into each other and hoping that your side had more men standing at the end of it

At the same time (and in no small part as a result of his training as an artillery officer) Napoleon shifted the emphasis from field tactics to the use of artillery. He noted while at the *Ecole Militaire* that huge advances were being made in metallurgy and canon development. The innovations by Jean-Baptiste de Gribeauval, with the introduction of smaller and lighter canon, allowed for greater firepower. This was not just confined to the heavy artillery divisions. It also enabled horse artillery to be more effective. The forerunner of the modern mobile artillery that we take for granted in the form of tank divisions found its earliest roots in the ability of cavalry to harness the greater firepower of the new small bore canons.

Theses advances in artillery, combined with the emerging military doctrines of Jean de Beaumont du Teil, who advocated the use of large scale artillery bombardments at the commencement of an engagement, and Guibert's writings on the use of speed in operations, coupled with De Bourcet's innovation of the smaller army unit, provided an astute commander with a revolutionary approach to military strategy.

The opening artillery barrage became standard practice. In the Napoleonic period. Battles commenced with massive heavy artillery barrages and then, under the cover of the smoke and carnage, the French infantry would move forward into position. Horse artillery would deploy with their smaller canon to a closer range and utilise 'grape shot' to take out further numbers of their opponents. Skirmishers would then surge towards the enemy and eliminate the command structure. While this was in operation the infantry would move ever closer as confusion spread among the leaderless opposition. Cavalry would split the opposing forces and allow infantry to pin one side and attack the other. A disciplined force approaching with twelve inch bayonets provoked panic and confusion.

These tactics had never previously been seen and were considered quite 'un-gentlemanly' at the time. They were, nonetheless, highly effective. The old system of marching into position and firing at the opponents infantry gave way to greater tactical deployment. The Corps system that Napoleon introduced confounded commanders who were still mired in traditional tactics. The strategy of the time was based upon a transformation and appreciation of the technology of the period and the capabilities of its different components.

Napoleon's first significant command over the Army of Italy was a model of ensuring organisational readiness and capability. At the time Napoleon assumed command the army was in a penurious state to say the least. It had been all but neglected by the government and existed solely for the defence of the southern areas of France, of which it was ill equipped and ill trained. When given the command of this rag tag bunch Napoleon immediately set to work to make it ready for what seemed like a hopelessly unrealistic objective. Some soldiers had no shoes or weapon, others ignored commanding officers and came and went with contempt, while others were at home with their families, yet apparently in active service.

Not only had Napoleon been charged with the command of this bunch of brigands but his plan was to cross the Alps into Italy and take on the might of the Austrian army entrenched in the fertile upper regions. The task was daunting for anyone let alone a young and inexperienced commander. Despite the difficulties Napoleon brought together the men into a formidable fighting force that not only successfully crossed the perilous St Bernard Pass through ice and snow but scored a series of victories that commenced the legend of Napoleon and the invincibility of the *Grande Armée*. Two things contributed to the ability of the Army of Italy to achieve its objective: it had the means and was prepared for the task ahead.

Contemporary relevance

Organisational readiness is the core requirement for being able to act effectively against competitors or to be able to enable service delivery. It is not enough for management to assume that these attributes exist. They must verify and ensure that it exists. Proposing grand visions are pointless unless the organisation has the capability and skills. The intention may be there but the organisation may not be ready to carry it out.

The assessment of organisational readiness is a key component of strategy. The fundamental issue is to give consideration to the circumstances under which the organisation is operating, assess the market, understanding the needs, and determine the most appropriate course of action. These factors are intrinsically linked. This type of analysis determines whether an organisation is in fact ready, and what needs to be addressed to ensure that it is.

Story in a box – Toyota

Although Japan did not seriously become a manufacturer or motor vehicles until the second world war it had produced its first vehicle as early as 1902. Until the advent of WWII the motor vehicle industry catered solely for domestic consumption but by 1945 it had been virtually wiped out. US forces had bombed most of the manufacturing facilities in Japan. Those that were still in business largely manufactured military machinery and had been shut down by the new US administration. US manufacturers quickly filled the niche and demand was met with a range of US firms exporting their product in greater numbers. It would have seemed at the time to any observer that the US motor vehicle industry would simply have Japan as another foreign market.

Thirty years later Japan was not only producing its own motor vehicle but successfully exporting them to the United States. Of the Japanese motor vehicle producers Toyota has firmly remained at the top. Its vehicles account for almost 50% of all motor vehicles sold worldwide and are more profitable than the three biggest US car markers combined[9]. How did a country go from virtually nothing to upstaging one of the largest and most established manufacturing industries in the world?

American occupation oversaw the revival of the motor industry and the first Toyota cars started rolling off the production line by 1947. Their vehicles were crude and cheap; basically austere, smaller copies of US vehicles. Exports commenced to the US in the fifties, and failed dismally. The US market was not ready for them and they were not ready for the US market.

Toyota went back to the drawing board. Keen to work out how to make their next attempt more successful they turned to several manufacturing experts from the

---

[9] The 'Economist'

US. One of these consultants, W Edwards Demming[10] became instrumental to Japanese success. His work had basically been derived from the experiences of the US during the war years. His other key contribution was the one factor that was sorely lacking – quality control. His philosophy was to embed quality throughout the manufacturing process. This gave the Japanese manufacturers an entirely different value proposition.

Toyota was the first to introduce what they refer to as the Toyota Production System (TPS). Based upon principles of 'just in time' manufacturing and Total Quality Management (TQM) the Toyota product made dramatic advances during the sixties and seventies. Quality control was rigidly adhered to, waste in the production process banished and efficiency pursued as the holy grail. For example, an engine from the US or Europe of that time was made from thousands of parts in 1960. Toyota reduced this to hundreds. Less parts equalled less chance for failure which resulted in greater production efficiency and greater client satisfaction. The manufacturing process was just one small part of the quality revolution. Quality was manufactured into everything right down to the sales brochures.

When Japanese motor vehicles reappeared on the international stage they were totally transformed. They were now reliable and economical. The fuel crisis of the seventies saw many people switch over to more frugal vehicles, and, to their surprise, they found them reliable, efficient and cheap to run. Japanese cars had established a foot hold and soon were able to compete equally with their American counterparts who had acquired a reputation for being thirsty, inefficient and expensive. It was now the US industry that had to go back to the drawing board to compete.

The Toyota Production System was a revelation. It not only enabled Toyota to compete with its more dominant rivals but helped it dominate them. Quality control became the mantra of the automobile market worldwide thanks mainly to Japanese production processes like that at Toyota. The process also allows Toyota to take advantage of new opportunities more quickly than its competitors. A new design can go from the drawing boards to manufacture in under two years. As a result Toyota produces a vehicle for any emergent market sector in a timeframe that allows it to capture the market before its competitors. The process does not stop there. Trends are fed back from customers to the design process so that the product is continuously refined.

Toyota hasn't stopped at improvement in just its production systems. What has become known as the 'Toyota way' is a culture unparalleled in the automotive sector. Employees are encouraged to propose ideas for improvement. Factory workers can stop the production line if they feel something is amiss. Everyone plays a part in the final product being a success. Even employees children come in to work and are cared for by the company. Workers are supported from 'cradle to the grave' and made feel part of something greater.

---

[10] Known as the father of the post war industrial revival in Japan

Through periods of troubled times in the motor vehicle industry Toyota seems to have weathered the tumultuousness. Toyota thrives because it does not rest on its laurels. Continuously looking for ways to make their products better and more suited to their customers, the focus at Toyota is on quality, employee welfare and the customer.

Two the key elements of organisational readiness are information dissemination and empowerment of individuals. When staff are informed they have 'buy in' to the organisation. Keeping people aware of what is happening throughout the planning process gives them a stake in the outcome. It is incorrect to assume that employees do not have the same vested interest or needs to know as management. If a secretive approach is adopted critical information can be misinterpreted and lead to false perceptions and rumour. Being kept informed empowers people and keeps them focussed and ready for emerging situations.

Information dissemination

It is becoming more commonplace in business for several parts of an organisation to contribute to a new venture, project or undertaking, sometimes several organisations as well. Who is in charge and what role they will play should be clear and understood by all involved. Without clarity of the processes and roles of people within the organisation can only lead to disaster. Hyperbole aside, one only needs to refer to the statistics on project failure rates and the cause of those failures to see that governance is critical to success. Good governance is about ensuring that processes are in place and that things are being done properly. An organisation and its component parts can only be deemed to be ready when the lines of accountability and responsibility are in place to determine whether it is or not.

Empowerment

The flat management structure heralded during the eighties was an attempt to break down the hierarchical model which had been the mainstay of corporate culture. The replacement 'open' style of working enabled staff at all levels to work together in a more collaborative manner. Management theorists advocated that it enabled a force multiplier effect where staff are able to perform functions that were traditionally the domain of management. Staff became more politically connected; allowing a composite picture to be formed, rather than a single point of view.

In the new millennium there has been growing awareness of worker autonomy and a reduced need for managerial oversight. Accompanying these changes has been an increase in productivity. At the same time governments across western democracies have noted a steady rise in workers choosing independence and autonomy. There is a greater awareness of the need to empower rather than control.

Summary

A group of people is only as effective as the tools and structures that they have to work with. Determining the state of readiness of any group to do the job is a leadership responsibility. The establishment of readiness cannot be devolved to others and it cannot be assumed. Knowing the capabilities of the organisation and being aware of the best means to employ your strategic resources is part of the skill involved in implementing strategy. Providing information to employees serves to engage and empower people, while at the same time maintaining transparency and trust.

Leadership tip

When you have determined your organisation's strategic resources make sure that they have the means to be able to deliver. The culture of an organisation should not act to inhibit the ability of its key areas to operate effectively. Determine what needs to be done and whether the organisation is able to achieve it. If not then take steps to ensure that it is.

Capability

The battlefield is a scene of constant chaos.
The winner will be the one who controls that chaos,
both his own and the enemy's.

N

The maxims...

Maxim XXXII

The duty of an advanced guard does not consist in advancing or re-tiring, but in manoeuvring. An advanced guard should be composed of light cavalry, supported by reserves of heavy, and by battalions of infantry, supported also by artillery. An advanced guard should con-sist of picked troops, and the general officers; officers and men should be selected for their respective capabilities and knowledge...

Interpretation: The selection of skilled and competent people for important positions is essential. Always ensure there is tight in-tegration between all parts of your organisation and that capa-bility and knowledge are high up in the assessment criteria.

Maxim I

The frontiers of states are either large rivers, or chains of moun-tains, or deserts. Of all these obstacles to the march of an army, the most difficult to overcome is the desert; mountains come next, and large rivers occupy the third place.

Interpretation: Every situation poses different obstacles to be overcome with varying degrees of difficulty depending upon the capability of your resources.

Maxim LXIII

All information obtained from prisoners should be received with caution, and estimated at its real value. A soldier seldom sees an-ything beyond his company; and an officer can afford intelligence of little more than the position and movements of his division to which his regiment belongs. On this account the General of an army should never depend upon the information derived from prisoners, unless it agrees with the reports received from the ad-vanced guards, in reference to the position, and composition of the enemy.

Interpretation: An organisation's capability is enhanced through intelligence but care should be exercised in determining the veracity of any information.

Maxim XLIX

The practice of mixing small bodies of infantry and cavalry together is a bad one, and attended with many inconveniences. The cavalry loses its power of action. It becomes fettered in all its movements. Its energy is destroyed; even the infantry itself is compromised, for on the first movement of the cavalry it is left without support. The best mode of protecting cavalry is to cover its flank.

Interpretation: It is imperative to know the capabilities of your organisation and co-ordinate them for maxim effect. Consideration should be given to the resources required across the organisation to support other parts of the organisation effectively.

Maxim LIX

There are five things which the soldier must never let from him: his gun, ammunition, knapsack, provisions for at least four days, and pioneering tools. Let him, if he thinks fit, have his knapsack of the least possible size, but have it with him always.

Interpretation: Ensure that you understand and provide the necessary equipment and facilities to people across the organisation. Care and concern for your people's needs should be a key consideration.

Napoleonic application

Eighteenth century Europe was rigidly stratified. The aristocratic regimes of the day were rife with nepotism and favouritism. Commanders of armies were generally titled aristocrats that treated warfare as a great adventure. Some military campaigns of the eighteenth century resulted in no bloodshed at all. Armies manoeuvred into positions so that the opposing force recognised that they would be defeated and simply capitulated.

All of this changed with Napoleon and the *Grande Armée* after the revolution of 1789. The fervour for the principles of liberty, fraternity and equality gave the people of France new purpose. Napoleon supported the ideals of the revolution and was very much in favour of a meritocratic system which supplanted the ideals of the *ancien regime*. Napoleon recognised talent and awarded it accordingly. One of his most famous sayings was that 'every soldier carries a Marshal's baton in his knapsack'; testimony to the belief that ability would be recognised and that all people had an equal chance to be successful.

The meritocratic system meant that those of talent rose quickly through the ranks. People were promoted by virtue of their efforts, and the army as a whole benefited. The French army saw the rise of the first professional Officer cadre. Every other nation chose their leaders on the basis of title and connection. The *Grande Armée* was open to anyone that had the ability to perform. This attitude pervaded the army and resulted in a highly motivated unit.

Story in a box - *corps d'armée*

One of the fundamental innovations that contributed to the success of the *Grande Armée* during the Napoleonic period was the introduction of the corps system (*corps d'armée*). Still in use today this reorganisation of the army ushered in a new style of warfare. Speed, movement and manoeuvre became the principles by which a successful army operated.

Prior to its introduction armies had basically consisted of a single homogenous composition with all specialisations in the one body. An army typically contained an infantry section, a cavalry section, an artillery section and so forth. These units were further broken down into even more specialised components such as skirmishers, *voltiguers*, grenadiers etc. The corps system allowed each corps to use its different components depending upon the strategy and tactics that it wished to employ for a particular battle. Each corps effectively became an independent army. The cavalry no longer remained an overall army unit but operated in each corps according to the dictates of that corps' commander. This meant that the army could operate as smaller, more efficient units allowing quicker operations. It also provided the capability to bring its force to bear as independent, intelligent units. The success of this innovation was proof positive in the way that Napoleon dominated the opposing armies of his time.

Despite being credited with the innovation of the corps system Napoleon was not its creator. Originally proposed by Marshal Broglie in 1761 during the 'Seven Years War' (1756-63) it was revived into military doctrine by Jacques Antoine Hypolite Comte de Guibert in his '*Essai général de Tactique*' written in 1772. Guibert's writings reiterated the findings of Broglie stating that an army should be composed of self contained divisions that allow them to operate independently with minimal supply. This work was followed by Pierre Joseph de Bourcet's, '*Principes de la guerre des montagnes*' (1775) which proposed moving in divided but well supported formations that could converge quickly on a foe. These were seminal works read by Napoleon and heavily influenced the way in which Napoleonic campaigns were conducted.

The smaller corps formations typically consisted of around 30,000 men. The composition of each corps was in effect a miniature army with all of the resources necessary to engage an opponent. The size of the corps enabled quick movement of men and material, so quick that Napoleon's enemies were often confounded by the appearance of what they initially assumed to be the main force. Enemy intelligence would estimate the approaching threat based upon presumptions about the movements of large numbers of men and materiel. If they calculated that the French would close in three days Napoleon would conduct an overnight march and close with the enemy in two. The effect was devastating. Napoleon's opponents were instantly placed on a defensive footing allowing Napoleon to seize the initiative. With their opponent off guard, the resultant engagement always placed the defending force at a disadvantage.

A well co-ordinated plan of movement of each corps meant that they could take strategic positions of their choosing. Napoleon employed the principle of 'march divided, attack united' which proposed that an army should march in separate units to force the enemy to deploy and be weakened by attempting to defend itself from a broad frontal assault. When the time was right his corps would give the impression of attacking the weakest point of their adversary to either force them to merge or to divide. Napoleon would then move into the breach and use his trademark 'pinning and envelopment' technique.

A somewhat humorous example of the lengths to which Corp commanders went to achieve their objective occurred in the Ulm campaign of 1805. The Austrian army had begun their incursions into Bavaria and were amassing in force around Ulm on the Danube. Napoleon had pre-empted the Austrian situation. The *Grande Armée* moved quickly to meet them. Marching orders were clear: two corps were given the responsibility of approaching the Austrians from the north, and two from the south and two from the west. In order to secure the southern approach it was necessary to cross the river Danube at the small town of Spitz. As the southern corps approached the Danube they were confronted by the Austrian army who had positioned itself at the end of a bridge crossing the river. Their position was formidable: the banks were lined with cannon and the Austrian soldiers were covered by steep river embankments. With no alternate avenue up or downstream with which to cross the French would be seriously delayed if the bridge could not be taken or if it was blown up by the Austrians. Under the cover of a peace flag the two marshals in charge of the corps, Murat and Lannes, walked onto the bridge. The Austrian commander, General Count Von Auersperg, somewhat intrigued by the audacity of the two Marshals, agreed to meet with them. Marshall Lannes then politely advised the Austrian commander that a peace had been formed between the two Emperors and that they were no longer at war. The Count accepted this and removed the cannon and retired. Two corps of French soldiers walked across the bridge with the full support of the Austrian army and proceeded to converge with the rest of the French army on the town of Ulm. When French cannon began its onslaught on Ulm old Count Von Auersperg suddenly realised that there had never been any peace and that he and the Austrians had been duped. The *Grande Armée* proceeded to surround the town of Ulm and all but forced the entire capitulation of not only Ulm but Vienna as well. As for the Count, he was imprisoned and later executed.

One of the items that Napoleon identifies in a soldier's pack is a pioneering tools. It seems obvious that a soldier would need his gun, ammunitions and food but the attention given to a pioneering tools is more than a passing reference. The pioneering tool kit contained the items necessary for operations such as digging, cutting etc One of the items added to this kit during the Napoleonic period was an entrenching tool. This was simply an axe-like instrument that could be used to gather wood for fires, help in building a shelter or forage for food. The rationale for it was to enable the army to live off the land and adopt a more independent means of operation. The previous means of constructing a shelter and starting a fire relied upon the supply wagons to provide the necessary materials and equipment. In effect the humble entrenching tool allowed soldiers to do it themselves and so units were able to move faster without being encumbered by a supply train. Similar principles can be applied in the modern context to act as an enabler for staff to be able to act more effectively. What these are is a matter for management to determine depending upon the strategy of the organisation. It is well worth considering what innovation your staff could utilise to gain a strategic advantage.

Contemporary relevance

An organisation's strategic resources are the primary means by which it is able to deliver and implement new initiatives. The capability to do so relies upon having efficient internal systems and processes. Without these elements the bringing together of resources becomes haphazard, and is more likely to result in delays, cost over-runs or failed implementations.

The interplay between strategy and other elements of an organisation was raised in the book 'In search of excellence' by Tom Peters and Bob Waterman with the '7S' model. It is not enough to simply regard an organisations strategic resources as the 'strategy, structure and systems', but to also incorporate elements such as 'shared values', the 'style of management' (culture), internal 'skills' and 'staff' capability. The role of the leader is to tap into these softer elements and ensure that the organisations resources are not being wasted because the other attributes of the organisation are not aligned properly with them. This might take the form of an organisation that has a strategic resource in its information technology but is hampered by a management culture that views technology with suspicion. Alignment across the organisation can only be achieved when all strategic resources are considered.

Story in a box – Supercentre Wars

The rise of the 'supercentre' almost wiped out main street. Everything from hardware to clothing has been subsumed into mega-stores like Kmart, Wal-Mart and Target. But it has not been plain sailing for these massive operations. A bitter struggle has existed between these organisations in an attempt to consolidate their position and prevent up and coming niche competitors from eroding their dominance. Wal-Mart initially emerged victorious as the market leader while Kmart ended in bankruptcy. What factors contributed to Wal-Mart becoming an outstanding success, and Kmart not?

Both Wal-Mart and Kmart opened their first discount stores in the same year, 1962 – Kmart in urban Garden City, Detroit, and Wal-Mart in regional Rogers, Arkansas. Both stores had embraced the discounting paradigm and operated along the same principle of 'lower prices – everyday'. The formula for success was similar and worked well with sales booming for the next three decades. A veritable explosion of discount retail stores occurred across the United States in the latter half of the twentieth century.

Even though both stores delivered low prices the difference was in how they did so. Wal-Mart tapped into the source of where cost savings could be achieved – the supply chain. It established a highly efficient inventory management system which basically allowed manufacturers and distributors to stock the stores directly. Kmart on the other hand relied upon their size and 'buying power' to negotiate the best deal. As a result their cost structure largely went unchanged. Meanwhile Wal-Mart was squeezing every last dollar out of the supply chain.

Kmart grew enormously during the eighties and covered almost every town across the US. It believed that it was unassailable and began purchasing other chains to increase its reach into the market. Attention turned to business expansion through acquisitions. Stock kept rolling in and filling the warehouses. After all, they were sure to sell it!

Wal-Mart on the other hand focussed on horizontal integration by establishing more cost effective supply mechanisms. Their inventory management system ('just in time' stocking) meant that inventory was on the shelves for the minimum time. Product lines were analysed to ensure that they were supplied in the most efficient and customer responsive manner. If something was selling well then stock was always available but if it was not then it was either dropped or supplied in smaller numbers. Wal-Mart went to the source of where costs could be cut. If a manufacturer could supply stock directly then the middle man was cut out. If a product could be sourced from a foreign supplier for less then the local supplier had to respond or be sidelined.

In the early 90's Wal-Mart decided to move into urban areas – Kmart's traditional territory. Kmart responded with the obvious strategy of simply undercutting them on price. Wal-Mart responded. Kmart retaliated and the price cutting war commenced. As margins were already slim on most product lines Kmart adopted the strategy of diversification into other more profitable lines (such as clothing) in order to minimise the impact on the bottom line of the cut-throat discounting. It was a good strategy: diversify into stock lines that had big margins to subsidise the slim margins from other products. Unfortunately for them Wal-Mart just kept going lower. Wal-Mart was able to dig into margins that Kmart just didn't have – the distributors margin. Wal-Mart could go lower because of efficiencies gained through rationalising the supply chain.

By the end of the nineties Kmart was in financial trouble. Unable to compete on price and with accumulating stock, profitability began to plummet. On top of this their buying spree of stores during the eighties that saw them diversifying into other market segments had left them short of valuable cash. The distraction from these non-core operations meant that they had taken their eye off the main game. When customers began abandoning the stores there was not much left but to file for bankruptcy protection. By the early part of the new millennium Kmart was closing stores across the country with its share price languishing at $3US. Wal-Mart's share price in the same period had quadrupled.

Why did Kmart fail? Quite simply because it did not have the internal capability to take on Wal-Mart. It relied on an outdated inventory management system and supply chain structure: two elements that are vital for retailing. Wal-Mart concentrated on improving every aspect of the supply chain and customer experience. Kmart diversified into other market sectors and lost sight of what was important at the local stores – quality, cleanliness and presentation. When Wal-Mart came to town it was not only able to compete more effectively on price but it also felt different, because it was different in presentation and in substance.

Clarity

Organisational capability is built upon the ability of the organisation to deliver what the customer needs but also the ability to remain viable. Establishing clarity around the components of a business that support these aspects requires in-depth understanding. It is curious that many organisations will have a defined list of what they expect from a new staff member but will not be able to articulate what elements make the business a success. Clarity around the organisational capabilities of the organisation can and should feed directly into the expectations of workers. A clear statement of their role and responsibility with respect to the organisations capabilities establishes a sound basis under which everyone can understand how they contribute. This forms part of the overall organisational capability and may be encapsulated in a document that outlines the structure and the roles and responsibilities of staff. This also serves as a means for staff to gauge whether they can perform in a higher role and so focus their attention on what they need to do to advance. There was a reason that Napoleon proposed that every soldier carries a Marshalls batten in his knapsack and that is because of the belief that every soldier has the capability to succeed.

Information

Every venture, investment or undertaking benefits from better information. Similarly, gathering information about the environment in which you operate is fundamental to success. In the military environment it is seen as more important than the size or capability of ones force. Sun Tsu (The Art of War) proclaimed that "every battle is won or lost before it is fought". Even though these words were recorded more than two centuries ago their significance has not diminished. The basis of this statement is that the party that has better knowledge of their enemies size, structure, morale, movements, location and so on will have a decidedly greater advantage. Throughout history the power of information has in many instances allowed an inferior force to overcome a greater one.

Gathering information and making use of it is necessary in order to be prepared and be in a position to make informed decisions. All sources of information should be considered and prioritised to form a composite picture of the situation.

Summary

Organisational capability is founded upon the capability of its resources. The strategic resources of an organisation are those elements that give the organisation its competitive advantage. Although the use and control of an organisation's resources is primarily a management function it still requires leadership to set the goal for how the organisation will utilise them. Every leader should therefore ask themselves: 'What are the things that my business or organisation needs to overcome and how would I go about it? These types of questions are supported by information gained about the market, an understanding of organisational capability and readiness to act.

Leadership tip

> *Differentiate between the resources in your organisation that provide it with the means to do business from those that give your organisation its unique character and customer value. Once you identify the elements of the organisation that give it the edge over its competitors then maintain the capability of these areas. There is no point increasing profitability if customer service and operational efficiency decline as a result; an organisation is an organism with each part affecting the other.*

Communication

The secret of war lies in the communications.

N

The maxims...

Maxim XI

To operate in directions far from one another without communication is a fault which usually leads to the commission of another. The detached column has orders but for the first day; for the next, its operation depend upon what has happened to the principal column; thus, according to circumstances, this column will lose time in waiting for orders, or more likely it will act at random...

Interpretation: Maintaining clear and effective communication across the entire organisation is vital to the success of any operation. Keep all parties informed and aware of what is required should be a priority of leaders.

Maxim XXVI

It is contrary to all true principles to make corps which have no communication act separately against a central force whose communications are open.

Interpretation: Where several parts of an organisation operate independently it is vital that communications be effective.

Napoleonic application

Communications has always been fundamental to the success of any military operation. The requirement for secrecy, combined with the need to inform has been a conundrum that has plagued military commanders for millennia. Napoleon's maxims do not provide a significant amount of coverage to communications in general but nonetheless identify it as essential for an army's success. The maxims cover two essential characteristics: ensuring that there is an efficient communication system, and that there is regular and consistent communication between all parts of the organisation. There is no great revelation in these observations but it is prudent advice that is more often than not taken for granted. If any organisation is to be effective then there needs to be effective communications among the components parts in terms of efficiency, regularity and consistency.

Story in a box – Wellington's secret

The defeat of Napoleon's army was something of a foregone conclusion following the Battle of Trafalgar in 1805. The reason being is that the English and allies could now go anywhere. Napoleon didn't appreciate the full gravity of the destruction of the French fleet at the time. After all, he was a land based commander. Napoleon's lack of attention on the navy is widely considered one of his fundamental strategic oversights. With the Royal Navy in command of the high seas following the destruction of the Spanish and French fleet England was free to go anywhere around continental Europe. As a result they were free to land troops on any part of the continent and with this type of advantage it was only a matter of time before the *Grande Armée* were fighting on multiple fronts, or surrounded.

In 1808 the Portugese had decided to reject the Continental system and allow English trade. Napoleon sent his armies into Spain to coerce Portugal back into the system. In response England sent an expeditionary force to support Portugal. Under the command of Lieutenant-General Sir Arthur Wellesley, later to become Duke of Wellington, the English were now in direct confrontation with the French. English troops freely entered the Iberian Peninsula unopposed by either French or Spanish navies.

The 'Peninsular War', as it became known, was a protracted campaign that drained France at a time when it could ill afford it. The depredations of the Spanish guerrillas, and the atrocities committed by the French grew proportionally intense as the war dragged on. Initially Napoleon was able to lead the armies required to beat back the English but with growing unrest in other parts of the empire he knew that he could not remain there to oversee operations forever. With the rest of Europe to keep in line Napoleon could not be fighting in the Iberian Peninsular and keeping his "allies" in check at the same time. His Army of Portugal eventually had to be directed remotely from Paris. As a result communication was vital; as long as he stayed in contact the Peninsular remained under French dominion and the English remained contained.

What the English needed was a way to remove Napoleon's imprimatur from the field of battle. The only way to do this was to intercept communications with Paris. The problem for the English was that the French had devised numerous means for ensuring that their lines of communication were unaffected. Correspondence was often carried in duplicate by several couriers, often disguised in many different forms. The main issue, though, was not so much the interception of the communications traffic but the deciphering of the encoded messages.

Military communications during the Napoleonic wars relied upon various forms of encoding to protect a message's integrity. The French had been using a technique known as a cipher for hundreds of years to protect the confidentiality of their diplomatic and military communications. The cipher was basically a system that replaced letters and words with a code. This code was based upon a 'key' that both sender and recipient possessed The increasing reach of the French empire made the requirement for an unbreakable cipher even more important to protect the communications that went to and from Paris throughout Europe.

During the Peninsula War the English had learned that the French had devised what was known as the *Grand Chiffre* (Great Cipher – also known as the Great Paris Cipher). This was seen as unbreakable. The Great cipher was a development on the previous incarnations by substituting even parts of a word or even letters from an enciphering table. The recipient would use a deciphering table and knowledge of the technique being employed to encode the message to translate it. A single word could have a variety of encoding methods. For example, the Spanish location of Seville could either be a single number (1359) or a string of numbers representing each letter or vowels (173.1085.521.90) or a combination of letters and bigrams. As a result the cipher table had tripled in size over previous incarnations, rendering it the most impregnable code to date.

In 1809 it appeared as though Spain and Portugal would fall into French hands with the defeat of the English at the battle of La Coruña. Wellesley returned to take command of the English troops in the Peninsula and gradually regained the initiative. Napoleon sent a string of marshals to oppose him with mixed success. Eventually the English army moved through Portugal and into Spain, and by 1813 it had crossed the Pyrenees and was on France's doorstep. The leadership of Wellesley was instrumental in the turnaround in English fortunes but there was something else that is not widely touted as the basis for his success - the English were able to read the Army of Portugal's coded messages.

During the Peninsula war English operatives had in fact broken the *Grande Chiffre*. By 1812 communications between Napoleon's armies in Russia through to Portugal were now legible to the English. They knew where and when Napoleon's marshals would move, the nature of their supply position, the morale of their troops, whether reinforcement would be provided, the route of their proposed retreat, and even their fears and expectations. This advantage saw England gain an ever increasing strategic position in the Iberian Peninsula and enabled them to eventually oust the French from Spain.

The Peninsula War marked the decline of Frances fortunes in Europe. For the first time in almost two decades the *Grande Armée* was seen as fallible. This revitalised the resolve of the continental powers and ultimately resulted in the end of the French empire. As astute a commander as Wellington or indomitable his soldiers the defeat of Napoleon was due, in no small part, to their ability to interfere with, and decipher French communications. With England's victory over the Army of Portugal by 1813, and the defeat of the *Grande Armée* at Leipzig by the continental powers in the same year, Napoleon's domination of Europe rapidly came to an end.

Contemporary relevance

Communication takes many forms and is not just confined to meetings, email or telephone conversations. Leadership establishes the manner in which communication is conducted and determines the culture that the organisation adopts towards it. In a hierarchical culture communications is generally linear and controlled but expected to be diverse at horizontal levels of the organisation. Whether this is the most effective structure for communication is based on many factors but these should be evaluated continuously as to whether they remain efficient and contribute to the success of the organisation.

Story in a box – Ideo

In the modern corporate environment innovation is a strategic multiplier. Every organisations needs to innovate or it will simply stagnate. One firm that specialises in innovation is Ideo. Ideo is predominantly a design firm that has developed into an innovation propagator. It has helped create over 3000 products, market leading products like the Apple 'mouse' pointing device, the first laptop computer and Palm V hand held computer through to the humble cycle drink bottle (*bidon*) and ergonomic toothbrush. These products have brought in millions in revenue and changed the way we do things. Ideo's list of clientele reads like the corporate who's who with BMW, Canon, Samsung, Prada and Nike to name a few. Ideo helps companies understand how to break out of the stifling inertia that plagues corporate cultures.

Ideo's success is largely based on harnessing the power of the group dynamic. Highly democratic, the culture at Ideo is to draw upon the combined talents of the many rather than rely upon the abilities of the individual. This may seem obvious but modern corporate culture still praises and rewards individual personal achievement and individual success. At Ideo employees are empowered to contribute their ideas at all levels of the organisation. Rather than a flat management structure Ideo employs a matrix where some people are managers of one person and subordinates in another area. The culture is collaborative and open.

Techniques that many organisations take for granted, or rarely use, are central to Ideo's success in product development. One of these, brainstorming, is more than just a communications mechanism – it's an experience. They even have a name for it – the Deep Dive. Its aim is to 'boldly go where no man has gone before' into the depths of the wellspring of creativity.

Ideo utilises brainstorming sessions to both bring out the creative impulses in individuals and flesh out the essence of the problem by drawing upon various approaches that different individuals have to a problem at hand. The sessions are conducted according to six core principles:

1. Defer judgement
2. Build on the ideas of others
3. Encourage wild ideas
4. One conversation at a time

5. Stay focussed on the topic

6.Visualise it

....

This process helps bring out the most in people and keep the sessions as productive as possible. The process helps refine what Ideo can provide for its customer and what the customers want, but more importantly, determine the underlying issues that need to be resolved. Armed with this information the process of engaging with the customer becomes more focussed and involved.

Ideo now helps organisations redefine themselves, improving internal processes and moving in new directions. The success of the Ideo method is based upon an understanding of interaction with their clients. They seek to understand what is really required and then bring to bear the knowledge and experience of different disciplines to cross-pollinate and spark innovation. Fundamentally Ideo is a success because it relies upon the power of communication both within and outside the organisation. It pulls together its greatest resource: the creativity and contribution of many, to identify solutions. This not only infuses people with enthusiasm but produces results. After all, the sum of the parts should always be greater than the whole.

Clarity

In order to communicate effectively in any organisation the type of information, channels and recipients of information must be clear. What needs to be communicated, where does this information need to go, and to whom are we communicating with or about? These may seem like basic criteria but there is often little clarity about what really need to be communicated in an organisation. There is also no clarity around whether something needs to be recorded (until it is too late). Leadership identifies what type of communications should be in place both within and external to an organisation. Are records of conversation for telephone calls required? Are emails to be stored? Should correspondence with external organisations be by letter only? These are but a small sample of considerations that need to be clarified to ensure that communications are relevant, necessary and effective.

Communication strategy

Establishing reporting lines and modes of communication is important to the governance of an organisation and also to ensure that an organisation remains accountable. A communications strategy is a mechanism that outlines the manner of communication in the organisation and the responsibilities of the parties to it. It can also cover stakeholder management including the types of internal and external communications required.

In order to facilitate good communications it is often a wise idea to prepare a communications strategy that covers all aspects of the organisation in different operating situations. A typical communications plan will have details of the parties involved and the manner in which communications should be conducted. The plan will also detail the requirements for meetings, escalation procedures for issues, and how different information is stored through document control.

The requirement to maintain good communications means that there needs to be processes in place to ensure that the appropriate communication takes. This may mean implementing a more 'open' style of internal communication or a more accountable type of external communication. Internal reporting should also be thought of in terms of how it facilitates the flow of information in the governance structure rather than simply as a perfunctory exercise to satisfy the need to prove that work is being done.

Communication is more than just the exchange of information. Recording and controlling communications and providing a suitable mechanism to provide clarity for all parties to the process provides greater efficacy and certainty.

Summary

Communication is the lifeblood of society and is no less important in any organised structure where human beings interact. The need for constant and effective communications is paramount to facilitate alignment across all aspects of an organisation. Communications both internally and externally needs to be established to maintain organisational control. A strategy for communications that is comprehensive and effective should be developed for an organisation, be it a corporation or a project.

Leadership tip

Always listen to what others have to say and then offer your opinion.

Too many people propose to have the answers without really understanding the problem.

More often than not the things that are not said are more important that the things that are, so try and find out what is really happening before acting. When you have decided on a course of action keep the organisation aware of what has been planned and how it is achieving it.

An open organisation is a healthy one.

Motivation

The men who have changed the universe have never accomplished it by changing officials but always by inspiring the people.

N

The maxims...

Maxim IX

The strength of an army, like the quantity of motion mechanics, is estimated by the mass multiplied by velocity. A swift march enhances the morale of the army and increases its power for victory.

Interpretation: Morale and confidence increase through purposeful execution. Decisiveness enhances the chances of success.

Maxim XV

Glory and military honour is the first duty a general should consider when he is going to fight; the safety and the preservation of his men is secondary; but this very boldness and tenacity ensures the safety and economy of life. In retreating, besides the honours of war, more men are often lost than in two battles; therefore, we should never despair, while brave men still remain with their colours, so we obtain – and deserve to obtain – victory.

Interpretation: A venture is more likely to be a success when people are invested in the outcome. Commitment to the cause will outweigh personal interest and ensure that people place the goals of the organisation first.

Maxim LX

Every means should be taken to attach the soldier to his colours. This is best accomplished by showing consideration and respect to the old soldier. His pay likewise should increase with his length of service. It is the height of injustice to give a veteran no greater advantage than a recruit.

Interpretation: One of the most effective way of maintaining peoples loyalty and commitment is to demonstrate that they will be looked after appropriately throughout their career.

Maxim LXI

It is not set speeches at the moment of battle that renders soldiers brave. The veteran scarcely listens to them, and the recruit forgets them at the first discharge. If discourses and harangues are useful, it is during the campaign; to do away with unfavourable impressions, to correct false reports, to keep alive a proper spirit in the camp, and to furnish materials and amusements for the bivouac. All printed orders of the day should keep in view these objects.

Interpretation: There is limited benefit from presentations and speeches in the early stages of an initiative Keep people informed and engaged during the process and this will have a far greater effect.

Napoleonic application

Napoleon saw one of his roles as a leader as providing for his troops and ensuring that their needs were being met. Any person taking charge of others should be acutely aware of their subordinates needs and provide for those needs accordingly. How often does anyone in a position of leadership ask what really motivates a person to do their job? In any environment it is all too easy to simply assume control and accept that the people will just do as they are told because they are trained to do so.

Napoleon had a keen insight into the hearts of men. He knew the qualities of a good leader and the power of good leadership. He provided for his troops and ensured that they were recognised appropriately for their efforts. It was well known that while Napoleon was a master of appealing to the hearts and minds of his soldiers he was also cognisant of their need for 'filthy lucre'. He appealed to what people wanted most (financial reward) while at the same time pandering to their higher aspirations (glory and honour).

Motivating people is not a once off act. While speeches have some effect they should be supplemented with actual involvement. The role of senior management distancing themselves is entirely contradictory to the manner in which Napoleon conducted himself in the field. Even as Emperor he was everywhere to be seen inciting and motivating the troops. The camaraderie that he built up among his men was legendary and often passionately expressed by his soldiers: during the parade attending his first abdication to Elba senior officers and soldiers cried – how many people would express the same emotion at your departure?

Story in a box – The *grognards*

As is the case for any military commands the relationship between soldier and officer is something of a love-hate relationship. This was no different under Napoleon. He affectionately called his old soldiers *grognards*, literally translated as 'grumblers' because they were always complaining. Able to withstand extreme privations these soldiers provided the backbone of the army. They were 'career soldiers' with most having seen action in numerous campaigns. Dependable, committed and redoubtable – they inspired the new troops that were recruited in ever increasing numbers. This alone was an important functions as soldiers were conscripted into Napoleon's armies as a result of the '*levee en masse*' proclamation following the French Revolution. The *grognards*, in particular, had little time for any commander that did not know what he was doing. The revolution had shown that title was something to be despised. If you had the ability and demonstrated it then you were likely to be followed.

Napoleon had an imposing impact on officers and soldiers alike - despite barely standing over five and half feet tall. Most of his men towered over him. Napoleon earned their respect because he led by example and swayed the support of the battle hardened by simply being one of them. In fact, on campaign, if he was accommodated in a palace or grand hotel he would still sleep in his tent. These types of facts became known by the troops and inspired them to consider him as being just like them.

Familiarity was also something that Napoleon did not shy away from. He was inclined to tweak his senior officer's ears, slap their shoulders or tap on people's heads. This created an environment where his Marshals vied for his attention and praise. A Marshal that received a slap on the shoulder was often regarded as being in the inner sanctum of Napoleon's elite. His officers often outdid each other not merely for pecuniary reward but the acknowledgement of being part of the inner circle.

During the Italian campaign the Directory awarded Napoleon one of the highest honours available for his success. Following the ceremony he asked his commanders to name the soldier that had demonstrated the greatest bravery during the campaign. A suitably brave *grognard* was identified and summonsed to Napoleon's tent. In an impromptu ceremony the soldier was then awarded the same medal by Napoleon himself. The effect of this could not be under-estimated. News spread throughout the army within hours and morale lifted dramatically. Soldiers saw Napoleon as one of them, someone that understood them and appreciated their efforts. It was no surprise that he was dubbed with the sobriquet 'the little corporal' as a sign of both respect and camaraderie by his army. He took time to know his men by name and made a point of being able to recall where they were from or what was important to them.

Why did his men follow him so devotedly? In the words of one of Napoleon's soldiers, Hendrik Van Loon:

'...Napoleon was the greatest of actors and the whole of Europe was his stage. At all times and under all circumstances he knew the precise attitude that would impress the spectators most and he understood what words would make the deepest impression – at all times he was the master of the situation.'

There was something inexplicable about why people so readily followed him. It was not just for riches, although these were often abundant; it was not just for glory, although this was always possible. He had a way of making people believe in a cause that was worth fighting and dying for. Napoleon was not only acutely aware of the elements required to deliver but was also focussed on the manner in which a leader should prioritise the needs of the country with his responsibility to his officers and soldiers.

Napoleon never lost the common touch and an ability to relate to people. He would often walk among the troops and 'hear their little stories'. He wanted to be a man of the people and was genuinely interest in the men that he led. He was a soldier and behaved like one.

Napoleon's speeches to his troops have been widely regarded as some of the most motivating of any commander. Despite this he believed that the most effect that a leader could make was during the campaign – in the trenches.

The final aspect of his style involved the use of force when warranted. Some occasions call for a strong hand while other situations necessitate deference. The art of being able to obtains your goals while still keeping others on side depends upon reading the situation and acting accordingly. On some campaigns if troops disobeyed orders they were disciplined harshly while others were praised and rewarded in grand style. The ability to do this to achieve the greatest effect required being in touch not only with the mood of the soldiers but also an awareness of the extent to which the system allowed the most appropriate reward or reprimand. It was a matter a balance and judgement.

Contemporary relevance

Determining what motivates people is a constant and often elusive challenge. While financial compensation is obviously important it has been widely acknowledged to not be the sole basis of what motivates most people. The challenge for any leader is to identify the things that motivate, and ensure that there is the ability for people to be able to achieve the goal set for them. In the business environment reward and recognition are the only real tools available but these are not the motivators that work consistently. Finding what motivates can be as simple as being understood and appreciated.

Story in a box – McDonalds

McDonalds trades in over 120 countries to an estimated 50 million customers a day. The stores are mainly franchise operations that are required to adhere closely to the McDonald's 'formula'. Despite receiving adverse criticism for everything from the nutrition of their products to the globalisation of American culture they remain at the forefront of their market segment and maintain a workforce that makes a product efficiently and identical to any store in any part of the world. It is no secret that this is all done by, predominantly, teenagers.

What motivates your average teenager today? A game console, a Tablet or the latest mobile phone perhaps. But give the same teenager to McDonalds and there is a wholesale transformation. They not only learn to cook but excel at it. They can serve hundreds of customers an hour with a smile. They even learn to organise other teenagers and take pride in their appearance. Does this sound like your child?

It is well known that McDonald's workforce average around 15 years of age. This is also about the same time when most teenagers suffer from the apathy and non-conformity that is manifested in their rebellious attitude. McDonalds doesn't just give them a job but gives them an identity that is almost totally at odds with their developing attitudes. It succeeds in the transformation by showing them what jobs are on offer and then asking them what they would like to do. It then gives them the responsibility to excel at that job and offers training programs that make any other form of training seem lame.

Training is accompanied by testing. Every employee must pass the testing for three areas of the business in the first month in order to remain employed. If you meet the grade then there are further options for advancement with the McDonalds Hamburger University as the pinnacle of customer service excellence. This state of the art facility covers every facet of the McDonald business. If your talent lies in making Big Macs then there is the option to compete to become the worlds best. This may sound cheesy (excuse the pun) but it offers the competitors an all expenses paid international travel opportunity that many teenagers see otherwise.

On the job, McDonalds encourages its managers to motivate the staff with a range of incentives. This can take a variety of forms from personal encouragement to being recognised as 'Employee of the Month'. Managers are also encouraged to develop an *esprit de corp* through strategic placement of people that are known to work well together. This is not just luck but good management. Bonds are formed between people that 'click' and have fun. Having fun is encouraged especially when it sometimes means cleaning the store after midnight.

But it doesn't just stop there. McDonalds is well aware that if you pay someone the same amount regardless of their productivity then you are unlikely to achieve any long term gains. Incentive schemes are backed up with real rewards that have relevance: everything from performance based pay to a company car for managers; from employee share schemes to personal loans, CDs, backpacks and a range of other items that are actually desirable – to teenagers. On your way to these incentives McDonalds makes no bones about allowing staff to eat what they want during their breaks (important to ravenous teenagers). The well run franchise becomes a small community.

One thing that serves to make McDonald's employees almost evangelical about the Company is the level of information provided. Employees are furnished with literature about every facet of the operation. Contrary to public perception most McDonalds employees know exactly what goes into the food. They become ambassadors for the Company and identify with the organisation. Staff are kept informed through employee bulletins, product disclosure documents and briefings. Far from being corporate propaganda the information is generally provided by third parties and suppliers as testimony to its veracity.

All of this leads to motivated and engaged staff that take pride in what they do, and at the same time enjoy doing it. There are not too many teenagers that have worked at McDonalds that will say that their time was boring, which is probably a testimony in itself. McDonald's has a system that works. They are still the worlds leading fast food retailer despite unrelenting criticism and adverse publicity. Regardless of what is said the fact remains that they produce one of the highest quality and most recognisable products in the world. It may not be gourmet, or free from fat or sugar, but then it doesn't pretend to be.

Think about this: if you asked an average teenager to make a hamburger without the McDonalds training, motivation and system what do you think you would get?

Incentives

Benefits are usually intangible: 'increased customer satisfaction', 'improved public safety', 'greater market share' and the like. This intangibility is not easily translated into something to which people can easily identify how their efforts will be rewarded. As a result there is little motivation from an incentive that cannot be tangibly recognised. It is for this reason that incentives need to be tangible. People need to be able to understand how their efforts contribute to obtaining a reward.

One way to address this problem is to ensure that objectives are crafted to be more specific and tangible. People can then focus on the achievement of the overall outcome by being able to achieve a particular objective. In the example of 'increased customer satisfaction', the objective could be 'reducing telephone waiting time on hold from 10 seconds to 5 seconds'. A simple system that measures the average time of hold and it can easily be monitored by the people that are trying to achieve the goal. The achievement of the goal acts as an incentive because people realise what they are expected to achieve in tangible terms.

Focussing effort on the attainment of an objective is akin to reducing the complexity of the problem to a smaller and more manageable component. While your role as leader is to focus on the big picture you still need to promote the smaller components so that staff can direct their energies to realistic and attainable goals and see that the rewards are also achievable.

Incentives should not just stop with the staff that bring in the revenue. All too often the only people that are provided with a monetary incentives are the sales staff. Support people are often not provided the same. If there is a reward system in operation in an organisation then it needs to extend to all people in that organisation. All too often management are provided financial incentives that the rest of the organisation regard as unfair. If one part of the organisation is motivated by financial incentives over and above their salary it is naïve to expect that everyone else in the organisation will not see this as a benefit. An incentive and reward scheme, if introduced, should apply at all levels, otherwise it may act as a demotivator.

The recognition and acknowledgement of individual effort is a crucial factor in motivation. The promise of rewards and benefits must be accompanied by sincere recognition of those achievements. One of the earliest examples of a motivational management model can be found in Douglas McGregors book 'The Human side of enterprise'. McGregor advocated that there are two different types of managers: those that believe that people need to be managed in order to achieve third party goals and those that would do so of their own accord if given the right motivation. The former type of manager see themselves as instrumental to people being able to perform tasks. The latter type see themselves as facilitating the means to enable people to meet organisational outcomes. These managers seek to align organisational goals with individual goals. Understanding motivators in your staff can help understand how to motivate.

Setting goals
Organisational goals and leadership visions can often be perceived as being too lofty and difficult to achieve. Leaders need to be able to translate organisational vision into something that people can achieve. The ability to break down an outcome into smaller components is essential if people are able to achieve 'short term wins'. For example, the management of an airline that proposes to become the dominant carrier on a certain sector may know that they have the qualities to achieve this but their staff may not be aware of how it is going to be achieved. If the goal is broken down into components, such as certain improvements to the booking system or customer service, then people will understand how they fit into the 'big picture'. It is this translation that makes the vision achievable.

Understanding how to go from the vision to the implementation is something that all leaders need to be clear on. This process was espoused by James M Kouzes and Barry Posner in their book 'The Leadership Challenge: How to keep getting extraordinary things done in organisations'. Their process for organisational improvement indicated that you must initially:

1. establish the manner in which the goal can be achieved;
2. set standards and create examples to be followed; and
3. break down the vision into realistic and achievable components.

At the same time it is necessary to inspire, motivate and encourage staff to follow the vision and build up a cadre of followers that will assist in pursuing the overall goals that have been set. Empowering others to act and creating an environment of trust and support is vital to achieving the outcome. The process also requires leaders to break down attitudes that impede the development of trust and support by giving people the ability to pursue new and better ways of working. The final stage of the process is to celebrate accomplishments and reward the effort being made. This is necessary because it is important to be aware of the extra effort that people make to effect change and the associated pressure that it imposes.

Reward and reprimand

Knowing how to adequately recognise and reward are key components for any manager's success but so are discipline and reprimand. In Ken Blanchard famous book 'The One Minute Manager' he identifies the need to conduct reward systems properly but to also reprimand properly. By this Blanchard advocates that people should be rewarded in such a way that it is not seen as vacuous, transparent or superficial. An award ceremony where staff are given plaques for performing a task when other staff were as instrumental in the process, or where the person being awarded has offset the effort with personal gain, will be seen as unwarranted and therefore devalue the 'award'. Reward needs to be for real and individual effort – if it is deemed necessary to separate the individual from the team.

Reprimand, on the other hand, needs to be for the *behaviour* and should not be personal. Reprimanding a subordinate will always be perceived as a personal slight so it is critical that it be directed at the action rather than the person so that you do not end up as the despised, unfair boss. Through rewarding and reprimanding subordinates you should always be perceived as just and fair rather than pandering or petty. The golden rule is that reward and reprimand should only be related to the action and never to the person.

Summary

It is a difficult balance to drive people yet be compassionate and understanding of their needs. Maintaining an *esprit de corps* so that staff remain committed is a tough day-to-day task that requires constant attention. Motivation is all important to achieving results and keeping people focussed. A balance between reward and reprimand is a difficult compromise. The simple things to remember are:

- Talk to people often
- Recognise and reward appropriately
- Be fair
- Address problems quickly
- Involve people in the process

Leadership tip

Every time you communicate with your staff remember that it will be viewed as a motivator or a demotivator. You may not think that you have as great an effect but you do. Always encourage feed back and include people as part of the solution. Take steps to develop and foster ownership.

Alignment

*Ten people who speak make more noise
than ten thousand who are silent.*

N

The maxims...

Maxim XLVII

*Infantry, cavalry and artillery, can never do without each other;
they should, therefore, be so cantoned as always to aid one another in case of surprise.*

Interpretation: An organisation is only as effective as its component parts. The greatest effect is achieved by leveraging off the
combined effect of your resources.

Maxim LXXXVIII

*Cavalry of the line should be posted in van, rear, wings, and re-
serve to support the light cavalry.*

Interpretation: Support your organisation with its strategic resources at all points. Complement your weakest elements with
the strong ones so that there is nowhere that an opponent can
infiltrate.

Maxim L

*Cavalry charges are equally good at the commencement, the mid-
dle, and the end of the battle; they should be made as often as
possible on the flanks of the infantry, especially when the latter is
engaged in front.*

Interpretation: Employ your resources with discretion to achieve
their greatest effect. Only through the correct application of the
right resources at the right time will success be achieved.

Maxim XCIII

*The better the infantry, the greater the need to husband it, and
support it by good batteries. Good infantry is without doubt the
backbone of an army, but if it has had to fight for some length of
time against very superior artillery, it will be demoralized and destroyed. It may be that a general, a more skilful manoeuvrer than
his opponent, may, with his superior infantry, be successful in a*

part of the campaign, although his artillery is much inferior; but, at the crisis of a general engagement he will bitterly feel his weakness in artillery.

Interpretation: Avoid entering into any competitive situation without your most effective resources. Know the situation well and plan for it accordingly.

Maxim LIV

Artillery should always be placed in the most advantageous positions, and as far in front of the line of cavalry and infantry, without compromising the safety of the guns, as possible. Field batteries should command the whole country round from the level of the platform. They should on no account be masked on the right and left, but have free range in every direction.

Interpretation: Your organisation's strategic resources should always be engaged fully and not distracted by surrounding circumstances.

Napoleonic application

Napoleon may have been the right man at the right time but his success was more than mere serendipity. There was nothing revolutionary about the reorganisation of the army or the development of artillery. Any competent leader would have realised their significance. The real effect came from the use of the right resource, at the right time, under the right circumstances. To facilitate this engagements were precisely planned and co-ordinated. Nothing could be left to chance as chance, too often, overwhelms the greatest plan. The combined effect of the 'new' tactics that relied upon speed, manoeuvre and attack at a particular point or 'hinge' enabled Napoleon and his marshals to better leverage their resources than their opponents. The greatest victories were obtained through clever usage of these principles. When everything came together, as more often than not it did, the results were devastating but when it didn't...

Story in a box – The Battle of Waterloo (1815)

Many books have examined the basis of why Napoleon lost the battle of Waterloo. Whether it was hubris, poor timing or just plain bad luck is open to debate. Napoleon's account of why he lost Waterloo, in his memoirs on St Helena, basically ascribed it to a series of events that were simply beyond his control and comprehension. His apologists have contended that he was simply not in form that day but the reality of the situation was more a case that key factors were beyond his control.

Napoleon felt confident on the day of the battle, more confident than in many previous campaigns. Jaunting around the command centre Napoleon boasted to his commanders: '...Wellington is a bad General, the English are bad troops and this affair is nothing more than eating breakfast'. His plan was to commence the battle with the usual artillery bombardment and then an unimaginative frontal assault. The former being something that the English not only expected but prepared for by utilising the reverse side of the hill upon which they had assembled to shield them from the French artillery. The proposed frontal assault was hardly befitting Napoleon's reputation and military genius, but as he had met the English once before in the Iberian Peninsula he did not think that they would offer much of a contest. Unfortunately for him they had learnt much from that campaign.

Contrary to his own principles Napoleon chose to attack Wellington on a field not of his choosing. It had also rained heavily in the days preceding the battle which would militate the effect of the artillery to a great extent as the ground would absorb much of the impact. Wellington counted on the fact that the sodden ground would also impede Napoleon and take away his trademark tactics of speed, manoeuvre and seizing the initiative.

Napoleon was also aware of the effect of the rain and the sodden ground. Rather than manoeuvre he simply chose to delay the initial attack giving the English further time to prepare. In the meantime he hoped that the sun would dry the ground. It didn't. The commencement of the campaign saw canon-balls soaked up by the mud. Those that did reach the troops mainly went overhead. The French infantry trudged forward through the mud. Fighting became a slugging match with isolated pitched battles.

Rather than dividing the enemy and overwhelming each part in turn Napoleon found his men absorbed in a useless struggle over a local farmhouse. At nearby Quatre Bras the small farmhouse became the obsession of the *Grande Armée*. More and more men poured in to take a structure that served no strategic purpose. At the same time his greatest commanders launched attacks that were premature or without cover. Marshall Ney launched a cavalry charge without the support of the infantry and the English just 'formed square' and repelled them. The usual tactic was to have the cavalry charge and force the opposing infantry to form square which limited the effectiveness of their fire power. The opposing infantry would then move into position in a fully deployed line and open fire on the square. The transition from square to line made the troops even more vulnerable. But this did not happen at Waterloo. To compound the problem when infantry charges were launched they were without the support of the cavalry. The English had learnt that only with indomitable courage could they resist the *Grande Armée*. They stood their ground and fired at point blank range. Their courage unnerved the French who had been so use to seeing their enemies flee in the face of the greatest army in Europe.

If things were not going as expected on the battle-field they were not going too well off it either. Prior to the battle's commencement Napoleon had detached Marshall Grouchy to engage with the Prussian army so as to prevent them from joining up with the English. Napoleon detached a third of his forces for this purpose. When the fighting commenced Grouchy was positioned several miles away eating break-fast and could hear the cannonade that preceded the fighting. But his corps had not been able to locate the Prussians. With the battle now under way it would have been prudent to determine whether the directive to find and engage the Prussians was still necessary. While his officers incited their commander to return to Water-loo he simply replied that he was ordered to engage with the Prussians. In fact, during the Waterloo campaign Grouchy's corps did nothing at all – neither facing the English nor the Prussians. Napoleon was to later comment that it was as if the earth had opened up and swallowed a third of his army. The effect of this meant that not only did the Prussian's have unimpeded access to the battlefield but the *Grande Armée* was seriously down on manpower.

As the situation went from bad to worse the tactics simply became less imagina-tive. Frontal assaults up hill became the norm. Despite this there was not much between the two adversaries as the battle ebbed and flowed from one sides favour to the other. When the French sighted what they believed to be Grouchy and the vitally needed reinforcements the *Grande Armée* pressed the English to breaking point. As the approaching troops came into range they were identified – not as Grouchy's men but the Prussian army. French morale evaporated. The Prussian cavalry sliced through the flanks of the French lines – all was lost.

Mistakes by Napoleon and his commanders were rife on the day of the Battle of Waterloo. In a high risk and uncertain environment it is usually the side that makes the least mistakes that generally obtains the advantage. While the maxims contain the insight from the success of many battles they also contain the bitter realisation of ignoring fundamental principles. The Battle of Waterloo stands as a stark re-minder to anyone that the outcome of any situation is not only dependant upon the way in which it is planned but the control that is exercised during the imple-mentation.

Contemporary relevance

Organisational alignment is more than having the resources that are able to de-liver the organisations purpose. The systems and processes to be able to deliver must also exist. This is another area where leadership is necessary. Whether it be aligning the culture of the organisation to meet its purpose of providing the nec-essary systems and processes to be able to deliver, leadership needs to be knowl-edgeable and prescriptive. As a consequence it also needs to be aware of the components of the organisation and how they inter-relate. It is not enough to know that several parts of your organisation perform as expected without being aware of the performance of the non essential elements.

Story in a box – Chrysler Corporation

In 1979 the Chrysler corporation of America was almost bankrupt. There was no way to keep the doors open of a Company that had seen a continual loss of market share. In the face of both its local competition from the likes of General Motors and Ford, and the emergence of increasing foreign competition the end seemed inevitable. The Company had lost direction and was merely making products to compete with the 'big boys' but without any real focus or direction. It had burgeoned over the previous decades and developed a small army of a workforce that became increasingly more expensive.

Chrysler was suffering not merely from high production costs and low sales volumes but an uncertainty about who it was. They produced motor vehicles that competed with their rivals but they didn't really stand for anything in particular. Other manufacturers had iconic models that carried their image and identified them as something different. Their competitors continued to come up with new and innovative products. Not Chrysler. It was in debt and had no real image at all.

Into this rather gloomy picture came one of the most outspoken and determined business leaders in US history – Lee Iacocca. His task of rebuilding Chrysler and promoting its flailing Dodge and Plymouth vehicles was going to be a monumental achievement. On top of this the Company was in fact broke and required finance that no bank was prepared to provide. Tough decisions had to be made and the first order of the day was to set a new course for the Company.

The US was still in the grip of high petrol prices following the oil crisis of the early seventies. The large auto manufacturers were slow to adapt. Iacocca brought in sweeping changes that revitalised the manufacturing process. Large, fuel inefficient models were axed. The dawn of the medium sized compact car became the new way. Chrysler began focussing not only on new products but on an entirely new attitude to automobile design. Engines were made more efficient, cars were made of more cost effective materials and quality was rigidly enforced.

The realisation of what was necessary seems fairly simple in hindsight. US auto manufacturers made big cars that were being threatened by new, smaller and more efficient offerings from overseas competitors. Chrysler didn't compete with them but introduced vehicles that filled the niche between the two extremes. One of the first designs that turned around Chryslers fortunes was the Minivan. Like most other manufacturers Chrysler produced the ubiquitous delivery van. Like most other manufacturers Chrysler also produced station wagons as well. Both these vehicle types were large and thirsty. So Chrysler filled the gap with something that would appeal to the people that wanted something less family oriented than the station wagon and less commercial than the truck like van. It sold like hotcakes and set the trend that became the new market segment.

A successful product and new vision for the Company was an essential ingredient for turning around its fortunes but far more needed to be done. The old, unprofitable product lines had to go. This meant job cuts. Job cuts meant union action. It was bad enough that Chrysler was making losses and being propped up by government loans but to have a workforce that didn't want to work would be the final straw. Iacocca simply told the workforce that there were plenty of jobs but that they were only paying $17 per hour and not $20 per hour. To reinforce the dire nature of the situation he dropped his own salary to $1 to prove that he was genuine about the need to down size. The gesture demonstrated to all that he needed people that were prepared to make sacrifices for the chance of long term success.

With staff costs in hand and production lines more efficient the final piece of the Chrysler turnaround needed to come from the market. Consumers still needed to buy cars to keep the Company profitable. With a massive debt to be repaid and shareholders eager for a return on their investment the product had to sell in large numbers. The average US car buyer had to choose from an increasingly diverse array of products. How to convince people to buy the product of a failing Company became problematic. Again Iacocca came up with the approach that swayed the market to Chryslers cause. In inimitable fashion he taunted the market with the immortal quip 'if you can find a better car – buy it!' Customers not only gave Chrysler products a chance they realised that they were good. Once in the fold customer care became a Chrysler mantra.

The turnaround at Chrysler during the eighties and into the nineties was primarily attributable to Lee Iacocca. His infectious enthusiasm and drive permeated the Company. The company was given a new sense of purpose and was being led with a new *raison d'etre*. Iacocca became Chrysler and the staff knew it. In fact the staff at Chrysler even recognised the indelible mark that he left on the Company by ascribing a mnemonic to his name 'I Am Chairman Of Chrysler Corporation Always'. The leader of the organisation became both its champion and instrument of change. People followed because he took sensible steps and involved them in the process. A firm believer in talent and motivation he once famously said that he was not the smartest guy at Chrysler, but at least he employed him. Good people, good product and a focus on what the company needed to achieve were the essential ingredients for success.

Transformation

If the objective is to take and organisation in a new direction then it is likely that specialised resources will be required. The rationale for this is that specialists are generally more effective in achieving change. This is because staff are generally focussed on performing the day-to-day work that is required to keep the organisation running. Transformation involves the delivery of something that changes the business or produces some sort of innovation. The skills required to deliver innovation are distinct from the skills to perform day-to-day work. An organisation that make the mistake of diverting existing staff to innovation activities, and expect them to also continue with their normal work, is committing two faults at the same time: diverting staff to specialised work for which they are not best suited and at the same time the organisation loses resources that would otherwise be focussed on achieving organisational purpose.

Strategic resources

It is a commercial reality that every industry has its own idiosyncrasies. What makes a competitor more successful in a market segment is the way they utilise their strategic resources, that is, the resources that create the value proposition for an organisation. While most organisations contend that their people are their most valuable resource, they may in fact not be the resource that delivers the most value. For example, an organisation may have significant value in its reputation or perceived image, or in the technology running the business, or it may be the relationships and alliances that the organisation has within the market. Capitalising on the firms strategic resources and ensuring that they remain aligned with the internal operations of the organisation requires astute and well informed leadership. The consequence is that the organisation itself establishes leadership in the industry and maintains the link between its purpose and perception.

A US Study[11] conducted in 2000 analysed what made strategies effective and concluded that alignment within the organisational model is necessary to achieve a resultant benefit from the adoption of a new direction. It found that 'from over two years of targeted research ...the best firms successfully address competitive challenges not because they excel at any one thing, but because their strategies so effectively integrate market positioning with execution capabilities'. The alignment of the internal resources and capabilities of an organisation with the market expectation may seem like an obvious conclusion but is more often than not overlooked.

Summary

Strategy works when there is alignment between all of the components. Leadership is required to create alignment by bringing people together for a shared cause. Making sure that all parts of the organisation are aligned is an ongoing task that requires constant attention to detail. The objective of good organisational strategy is maintaining the organisations unique selling proposition or reason for being while at the same time capitalising on new opportunities.

In a nutshell alignment brings together the elements discussed in this section:
- Establish clear objectives,
- Effect planning,
- Determine whether the capability exists and whether there is internal readiness in the systems, processes and people,
- Communicate the objective and plan,
- Motivate people to achieve,
- Keep everything together.

---

[11] Strategic Integration: competing in the age of capabilities (Fuchs et al), California Management Review, 2000.

Leadership tip

Disorder is the natural state of any system. Only through constant attention to improving processes, systems and resources can the whole organisation improve.

Conclusion – final word

Despite all the accolades and glorification, Napoleon was not perfect, and while this book has lauded his maxims and the resulting traits it is recognised that his failures were as grand as his successes. What has remained though is an image of a person that defies simple analysis. His meteoric rise through the army and ultimately as the head of state could have been a fable and has ultimately become legend. It is true that in many instances Napoleon created his own legend in a time when control over the media was still possible. Nonetheless his military successes speak for themselves as does his ability to succeed in an environment where others failed. There is probably few other instances of any person in history rising on the back of success and dominating his sphere of influence so totally.

At this point the reader might assume that the book paints the definitive picture of leadership character and action. It doesn't. It identifies the attributes that emanate from the maxims and nothing more. Should anyone in a leadership role, or with leadership aspirations emulate Napoleon? After all didn't he lose the war?

How you apply the attributes that have been identified is a matter of discretion. As with any work on an imperfect subject the contribution is a part of a developing body of knowledge.

In 1833, Lord Holland, speaking in the English House of Peers, spoke about Napoleon in these terms: 'The very people who detested this great man have acknowledged that for ten centuries there has not appeared upon earth a more extraordinary character.'

There is nothing astounding about leadership, we can all be leaders. You will find an endless array of theories and texts to explain what works and what doesn't but in the end there are no complex processes to be followed, just your own internal beliefs and convictions. Perhaps the most significant advice for anyone wanting to lead others is that of the father of Taoism, Chinese philosopher Lao Tsu, born over 300 years before Christ:

> To lead people, walk beside them ...
> As for the best leaders, the people do not notice their existence.
> The next best, the people honour and praise.
> The next, the people fear;
> and the next, the people hate ...
> When the best leader's work is done the people say,
>
> "We did it ourselves!"

Appendix – The complete military maxims

The following interpretations have been taken from 'Napoleon's military maxims' by General Sir George D'Aguillar and 'Napoleon's little red book' by John McErlean. The maxim used have the annotation of GD or JM, respectively, after it to indicate its source.

Maxim I

The frontiers of states are either large rivers, or chains of mountains, or deserts. Of all these obstacles to the march of an army, the most difficult to overcome is the desert; mountains come next, and large rivers occupy the third place.
    GD

Maxim II

In forming the plan of a campaign, it is requisite to foresee everything the enemy may do, and to be prepared with the necessary means to counteract it. Plans of campaign may be modified ad infinitum according to the circumstances, the genius of the General, the character of the troops, and the features of the country
    GD

Maxim III

An army which undertakes the conquest of a country has its two wings either resting upon neutral territories, or upon great natural obstacles, such as rivers or chains of mountains. It happens in some cases that only one wing is so supported, and in the others that both are exposed. In the first instance cited, namely where both wings are protected, a general has only to guard against being penetrated in front. In the second, where one wing only is supported, he should rest upon the supported wing. In the third, where both wings are exposed, he should depend upon a central formation, and never allow the different corps under his command to depart from this; for it be difficult to contend with the disadvantage of having two flanks exposed, the inconvenience is doubled by having four, tripled if there be six; that is to say, if the army is divided into two or three different corps. In the first instance then, as above quoted, the line of operation may tend indifferently to the right or to the left. In the second, it should be directed to the wing in support. In the third it should be perpendicular to the centre of the army's line of march. But in all these cases it is necessary every five or six days to have a strong post,

or an entrenched position, upon the line of march, in order to col-
lect stores and provisions, to organise convoys, to form a centre
of movement, and establish a point of defence, to shorten the line
of operations.
GD

Maxim IV

When the conquest of a country is undertaken by two or three
armies, which have each their separate lines of operation, until
they arrive at a point fixed upon for their concentration, it should
be laid down as a principle, that the junction should never take
place near the enemy, because the enemy, in uniting his forces,
may not prevent it, but beat the armies in detail.
GD

Maxim V

All war should be methodical, for every war should have an aim,
and be constructed in accordance with the principles and rules of
art. It should be carried on with means proportional to the obsta-
cles which can be foreseen.
JM

Maxim VI

At the commencement of a campaign, to advance or not to ad-
vance is a matter for grave consideration, but when once the of-
fensive has been assumed, it must be sustained to the last
extremity. However skilful the manoeuvres, a retreat will always
weaken the morale of an army, because in losing the chances of
success these last are transferred to the enemy. Besides, retreat
cost always more men and materiel than the most bloody en-
gagement; with this difference, that in a battle the enemy's loss
is nearly equal to your own, whereas in a retreat the loss is on
your side only.
GD

Maxim VII

An army should always, night and day, and in any hour, be pre-
pared to offer all the resistance of which it is capable; and this
demands that the troops should constantly have with them their
arms and ammunition, the infantry with its artillery, cavalry and
generals; that the different divisions of the army should be con-
stantly in a position to support, sustain, and protect one another;

that whether in camp, on the march, or at the halt, the troops should be always in a position of vantage, which has the qualities necessary for every battle-field, i.e., that the flanks should be well supported, and that all weapons should be placed in the most advantageous position to be brought into immediate play. When the army is en route there should always be scouts in front and to the right and left, to give information, and placed at such a distance, that the main body of the army may deploy and take up its position unmolested.

JM

Maxim VIII

A general-in-chief should say to himself during the day: "If the enemy's army were to appear on my front, or on my right or on my left, what would I do?" And if he finds the question hard to answer, he is not properly posted, things are not well ordered, and he must put matters right, and at once.

JM

Maxim IX

The strength of an army, like the quantity of motion mechanics, is estimated by the mass multiplied by velocity. A swift march enhances the morale of the army and increases its power for victory.

JM

Maxim X

When an army is inferior in number, inferior in cavalry, and in artillery, it is essential to avoid a general action. The first deficiency should be supplied by rapidity of movement; the want of artillery by the nature of the manoeuvres; and the inferiority in cavalry by the choice of position. In such circumstances the morale of the soldier does much.

GD

Maxim XI

To operate in directions far from one another without communication is a fault which usually leads the commission of another. The detached column has orders but for the first day; for the next, its operation depend upon what has happened to the principal column; thus, according to circumstances, this column will lose time in waiting for orders, or more likely it will act at random. It ought to be then a principle that an army should have all its columns together, so that the enemy could find no possible means of getting in between them: When, for any reasons whatever, this maxim is departed from, it is necessary that the detached bodies should independent in their operations; they should bear on to fixed point where they are to assemble; they should march without hesitation and without new orders; finally, they should be as little as possible subject to isolated attack.

JM

Maxim XII

An army ought only to have one line of operation. This should be preserved with care, and never abandoned but in the last extremity.

GD

Maxim XIII

The distances permitted between the corps of an army upon the march must be governed by the localities, by circumstances, and by the object in view.

GD

Maxim XIV

Among mountains, a great number of positions are always to be found very strong in themselves, and which it is dangerous to attack. The character of this mode of warfare consists in occupying camps on the flanks or in the rear of the enemy, leaving him only the alternative of abandoning his position without fighting, to take up another in the rear, or to descend from it in order to attack you. In mountain warfare the assailant always has the disadvantage. Even in offensive warfare in the open field the great secret consists of defensive combats, and in obliging the enemy to attack

GD

Maxim XV

Glory and military honour is the first duty a general should consider when he is going to fight; the safety and the preservation of his men is secondary; but this very boldness and tenacity ensures the safety and economy of life. In retreating, besides the honours of war, more men are often lost than in two battles; therefore, we should never despair, while brave men still remain with their colours, so we obtain – and deserve to obtain – victory.

JM

Maxim XVI

It is an approved maxim of war, never to do what the enemy wishes you to do, for this reason alone, that he desires it. A field of battle, therefore, which he has previously studied and reconnoitred, should be avoided, and double care should be taken where he has had time to fortify and entrench. One consequence deducible from this principle is, never to attack a position in front which you can gain by turning.

GD

Maxim XVII

In a war of march and manoeuvre, if you would avoid a battle with a superior army, it is necessary to entrench every night, and occupy a good defensive position. Those natural positions which are ordinarily met with, are not sufficient to protect an army against the superior numbers without recourse to art.

GD

Maxim XVIII

Surprised by a superior force, an ordinary general occupying a bad position would seek safety in retreat; but a good commander will put a bold face on it and march to meet the foe. By such action he disconcerts his opponent, and, if the latter shows any irresolution in his march, a skilful general, profiting by this moment of indecision, may even hope for victory, or at least gain the day by manoeuvring; at night he can entrench himself or fall back on a better position. By such bold action he maintains the honour of war, that important essential in the strength of an army.

JM

Maxim XIX

The transition from the defensive to the offensive is one of the most delicate operations in war.

JM

Maxim XX

We should not abandon our line of operations; but it is one of the most skilful manoeuvres in the art of war to be able to change it when circumstances authorize it. An army which changes skillfully its line of operation deceives the foe, who no longer knows its rear and its weak points.

JM

Maxim XXI

When an army carries with it a battering train, or large convoys of sick and wounded, it cannot march by too short a line upon its depots.

GD

Maxim XXII

The art of camping on a position is the same as the forming of a line of battle on this position. To do this, all arms should be favourably placed in order to be brought into action; we should choose a position which is not commanded and which cannot be turned; and, if it be possible, it should command and envelop the enemy's position.

JM

Maxim XXIII

*When you are occupying a position which the enemy threatens to surround, collect all your force immediately, and menace **him** with an offensive movement. By this manoeuvre you will prevent him from detaching and annoying your flanks, in case you should judge it necessary to retire.*

GD

Maxim XXIV

Never lose sight of this maxim, that you should establish your cantonments at the most distant and best protected point from the enemy, especially where a surprise is possible. By this means you will have time to unite all your forces before he can attack you.

GD

Maxim XXV

When two armies are in order of battle, and one has to retire over a bridge, while the other has the circumference of the circle open, all the advantages are in favour of the latter. It is then a general should show boldness, strike a decided blow, and manoeuvre upon the flanks of his enemy. The victory is in his hands.

GD

Maxim XXVI

It is contrary to all true principle to make corps which have no communication act separately against a central force whose communications are open.

GD

Maxim XXVII

When one is driven from a first position, it is well to rally one's columns sufficiently to the rear to prevent the enemy interposing, for nothing could be more untoward for columns to be attacked separately before their junction.

JM

Maxim XXVIII

A detachment must not be made on the eve of battle, for in the night the situation may change - either by movements of the enemy towards retreat, or by the arrival of large reinforcements which allow it even to take the offensive and render the premature dispositions made, futile.

JM

Maxim XXIX

When you have the resolve to fight a battle, collect your whole force, dispense with nothing. A single battalion sometimes decides the day.

GD

Maxim XXX

Nothing is more rash and contrary to the principles of war than to make a flank march before an army in position, especially when this army occupies heights, below which it is necessary to defile.

JM

Maxim XXXI

Secure yourself all possible chances of success when you decide to deliver an important engagement, especially when you are dealing with a great general, for if you are beaten, and you are in the midst of your magazines, and close to your fortress, woe to the conquered!

JM

Maxim XXXII

The duty of an advanced guard does not consist in advancing or retiring, but in manoeuvring. An advanced guard should be composed of light cavalry, supported by reserves of heavy, and by battalions of infantry, supported also by artillery. An advanced guard should consist of picked troops, and the general officers; officers and men should be selected for their respective capabilities and knowledge. A corps deficient in instruction is only an embarrassment to an advanced guard.

GD

Maxim XXXIII

It is contrary to the usages of war to let one's parks and heavier pieces of artillery enter a defile if the other end is not held also; in case of retreat they will be in the way and be lost. They should be left ready, and under a suitable escort until mastery is obtained of the outlet.

JM

Maxim XXXIV

It should be held as a maxim to have no intervals between the different bodies forming the line of battle, unless it be done to get the enemy into a trap.

JM

Maxim XXXV

The camps of an army should be so pitched as to be a protection to one another.

JM

Maxim XXXVI

When the enemy's army is covered by a river, upon which he holds several têtes de pont, do not attack in front. This would divide your force and expose you to be turned. Approach the river in echelon of columns, in such manner that the leading column shall be the only one that the enemy can attack, without offering you his flank. In the meantime let your light troops occupy the bank, and when you have decided the passage, rush upon it and fling across your bridge. Observe that the point of passage should be always at a distance from the leading echelon, in order to deceive the enemy.

GD

Maxim XXXVII

As soon as one is master of a position commanding the opposite bank facilities are acquired for effecting the crossing of the stream, especially if this position is of sufficient extent to hold a large number of pieces of artillery. This advantage is less when the stream is more than 600 yards wide, for, the grape shot not reaching the other side, the troops resisting the passage can easily march past and shelter themselves from fire. It would come to this: that the grenadiers who are ordered to cross the river, to protect the construction of the passage, might reach the other bank, but would then be crushed by the enemy's fire, since their batteries, placed at a distance or 400 yards from the outlet of the bridge, would be able to open a very murderous fire, and yet be more than 1,000 yards distant from the batteries of the army wishing to pass over; so that the whole advantage in artillery lies on their side. In this case, too, the passage is impossible, unless it be by a successful surprise, or through the protection of an intervening island, or by taking advantage of a very pronounced bend, which would permit the establishment of batteries crossing their fires on the gorge. This isle or bend forms then a natural tete-de-pont, and gives the advantage to the attacking army. When a river is less than 120 yards broad, and a command is obtained of the opposite bank, the troops who have been landed on the other side, being under the protection of artillery, are so advantageously placed that, unless the river makes a bend, it is impossible for the enemy to prevent the establishment of the bridge. The bridge being a defile, a semi-circle should be formed about its extremity, and the army must march past the fire of the opposite sides at a distance of 600 or 800 yards.

JM

Maxim XXXVIII

It is difficult to prevent an enemy, supplied with pontoons, from crossing a river. When the object of an army which defends the passage is to cover a siege, the moment the General has ascertained his inability to oppose the passage, he should take measures to arrive before the enemy, at an intermediate position between the river he defends and the place he desires to cross.

GD

Maxim XXXIX

In the campaign of 1645 Turenne was attacked with his army before Philipsburg by a very superior force. There was no bridge here over the Rhine, but he took advantage of the ground between the river and the place to establish a camp. This should serve as a lesson to the engineering officers, not merely in the construction of fortresses, but of têtes de pont. A space should always be left between the fortress and the river, where an army may form and rally without being obliged to throw itself into the place, and thereby compromise its security. An army retiring upon Mayence before a pursuing enemy is necessarily compromised; for this reason, because it requires more than a day to pass the bridge, and because the lines of Cassel are too confined to admit any army to remain there without being blocked up. Two hundred toises should have been left between that place and the Rhine. It is essential that all têtes de pont before great rivers should be constructed upon this principle, otherwise they will prove a very inefficient assistance to protect the passage of the retreating army. Têtes de pont, as laid down in our schools, are of use only for small rivers, the passage of which is comparatively short
  GD.

Maxim XL

Strong places are useful in offensive as in defensive war. They could not indeed stop the advance of an army, but they offer excellent means of delaying, checking, weakening, and harassing a victorious enemy.
  JM

Maxim XLI

There are but two ways of effectually besieging a place, one by first defeating the hostile army entrusted with the duty of covering it and driving the remnants beyond some natural obstacle, e.g., mountains, or a great river; the covering force being removed, an observing army must be placed behind the natural obstacle, until the siege-works are completed and the place taken. But if it is desired to take the place in face of a reinforcing army without the risk of a battle, one must be provided with a siege-train, with ammunition and provisions, for the expected duration of a siege, and lines of contravallation and circumvallation, taking advantage of localities such ail heights, woods, marshes, inundations. there being no need to maintain communication with the depot posts, there is only need to keep the relieving army in check; in this case an observing army should be formed to keep an eye on the relief force, and bar its way to the place, by means of which it is always possible to attack it in the flank or rear if it attempts to steal a march; by taking advantage of the lines of circumvallation, a part of the place a body four times the garrison, to number yet an equal figure with the army of relief, it may be more than one march distant; if after this detachment it be inferior in number, it should be but a short march from the siege, in order to be able to fall back on its lines, or rather, to receive reinforcements in case of attack. If the two armies engaged in the siege and in observation together are but equal to the relieving force, the whole of the besieging army should remain in or near the lines, and confine itself to pushing forward the siege operations with all the vigour possible.

JM

Maxim XLII

Feuquieres has said you are never to wait for the enemy within the lines of circumvallation; but sally out and attack him. Feuquieres is wrong; there is no dogmatic rule in war, nor should there be one against waiting for the foe within the lines.

JM

Maxim XLIII

Those who would reject lines of circumvallation and all the assistance the engineers' art can afford, deprive themselves gratuitously of an aid which is never hurtful, almost always useful, and often indispensable. However, the principles of field fortification have made no progress since the time of the ancients; it is even below what it was 2,000 years ago. Encouragement then should be given to officers of talent to perfect this part of their art, and to bring it to the same level with the others.

JM

Maxim XLIV

Circumstances not permitting that a sufficiently large garrison should be left behind to defend a fortress containing hospital and stores, all measures should be taken to secure the citadel from being stormed.

JM

Maxim XLV

A fortified place can only protect the garrison and arrest the enemy for a certain time. When this time has elapsed and the defences are destroyed, the garrison should lay down its arms. All civilised nations are agreed on this point, and there never has been an argument except with reference to the greater or lesser degree of deference which a governor is bound to make before he capitulates. At the same time there are generals, Villars among the number, who are of the opinion that a governor should blow up the fortifications, and take advantage of the night to cut his way through the besieging army. Where he is unable to blow up the fortifications, he may always retire, they say, with his garrison, and save the men. Officers who have adopted this line of conduct have often brought off three-fourths of their garrison.

GD

Maxim XLVI

The keys of a fortress are well worth the retirement of a garrison, when it is resolved to yield only on those conditions. On this principle it is always wiser to grant an honourable capitulation to a garrison which has made a vigorous resistance than to risk an assault.

GD

Maxim XLVII

Infantry, cavalry and artillery, can never do without each other; they should, therefore, be so cantoned as always to aid one another in case of surprise.

JM

Maxim XLVIII

The formation of infantry in line should be always in two ranks, because the length of the musket only admits of an effective fire in this formation. The discharge of the third rank is not only uncertain, but frequently dangerous to the ranks in its front. In drawing up infantry in two ranks, there should be a supernumerary behind every fourth or fifth file. A reserve should likewise be placed twenty-five places in rear of each flank.

GD

Maxim XLIX

The practice of mixing small bodies of infantry and cavalry together is a bad one, and attended with many inconveniences. The cavalry loses its power of action. It becomes fettered in all its movements. Its energy is destroyed; even the infantry itself is compromised, for on the first movement of the cavalry it is left without support. The best mode of protecting cavalry is to cover its flank.

GD

Maxim L

Cavalry charges are equally good at the commencement, the middle, and the end of the battle; they should be made as often as possible on the flanks of the infantry, especially when the latter is engaged in front.

JM

Maxim LI

It is for the cavalry to follow up the beaten enemy and prevent his rallying.

JM

Maxim LII

Artillery is more essential to cavalry than to infantry, because cavalry has no fire for its defence, but depends upon the sabre. It is to remedy this deficiency that recourse has been had to horse artillery. Cavalry, therefore should never be without cannon, whether when attacking, rallying, or in position.

GD

Maxim LIII

In march or in position the greater part of the artillery should be with the division of infantry and cavalry. The rest should be in reserve. Each gun should have three hundred rounds, without including the limber. This is about the complement for two battles.

GD

Maxim LIV

Artillery should always be placed in the most advantageous positions, and as far in front of the line of cavalry and infantry, without compromising the safety of the guns, as possible. Field batteries should command the whole country round from the level of the platform. They should on no account be masked on the right and left, but have free range in every direction.

GD

Maxim LV

A general should never put his army into cantonments when he has the means of collecting supplies of forage and provisions, and of thus providing for the wants of the soldier in the field.

GD

Maxim LVI

A good General, a well organised system, good instruction, and severe discipline, aided by effective establishments, will always make good troops, independently of the cause for which they fight. At the same time, a love of country, a spirit of enthusiasm, and a sense of national honour, will operate upon young soldiers with advantage.

GD

Maxim LVII

When a nation is without establishments and a military system, it is very difficult to organise an army.

GD

Maxim LVIII

The first quality of a soldier is fortitude in enduring fatigue and hardship; bravery but the second. Poverty, hardship and misery, are the school of the good soldier.

JM

Maxim LIX

There are five things which the soldier must never let from him: his gun, ammunition, knapsack, provisions for at least four days, and pioneering tools. Let him, if he thinks fit, have his knapsack of the least possible size, but have it with him always.

JM

Maxim LX

Every means should be taken to attach the soldier to his colours. This is best accomplished by showing consideration and respect to the old soldier. His pay likewise should increase with his length of service. It is the height of injustice to give a veteran no greater advantage than a recruit.

GD

Maxim LXI

It is not set speeches at the moment of battle that renders soldiers brave. The veteran scarcely listens to them, and the recruit forgets them at the first discharge. If discourses and harangues are useful, it is during the campaign; to do away with unfavourable impressions, to correct false reports, to keep alive a proper spirit in the camp, and to furnish materials and amusements for the bivouac. All printed orders of the day should keep in view these objects.

GD

Maxim LXII

Tents are unfavourable to health. The soldier is best when he bivouacs, because he sleeps with his feet to the fire, which speedily dries the ground on which he lies. A few planks and a morsel of straw shelter him from the wind. On the other hand tents are necessary for the superior officers, who have to write and consult their maps. Tents should therefore be issued to these, with directions to them never to sleep in a house. Tents are always objects of observation to the enemy's staff. They afford information of your numbers, and the ground you occupy, while an army bivouacking in two or three lines is only distinguishable from afar by the smoke which mingles with the clouds. It is impossible to count the number of the fires.

GD

Maxim LXIII

All information obtained from prisoners should be received with caution, and estimated at its real value. A soldier seldom sees anything beyond his company; and an officer can afford intelligence of little more than the position and movements of his division to which his regiment belongs. On this account the general of an army should never depend upon the information derived from prisoners, unless it agrees with the reports received from the advanced guards, in reference to the position, and composition of the enemy.

GD

Maxim LXIV

Nothing is more important in war than unity in the command; thus when there is war against but one power there should be but one army, acting on one line, and by one chief.

JM

Maxim LXV

The same consequences which have uniformly attended long discussions and councils of war will follow at all times. They will terminate in the adoption of the worst course, which in war is always the most timid, or, if you will, the most prudent. The only true wisdom in a General is determined courage.

GD

Maxim LXVI

In war, the leader alone understands the importance of certain things, and he alone, of his own will and superior wisdom, conquers and overcomes all difficulties.

JM

Maxim LXVII

Allowing generals and officers to lay down arms, as the result of a particular capitulation, except when they form the garrison of a fortified place, leads the way to undeniable difficulties. It is destructive to the military spirit of a nation thus to open a way to cowardly or timid men, or even to brave men who have strayed. In an extraordinary position, extraordinary resolution is needed; the more important the resistance of any body, the better are its chances of being succoured or of cutting its way through. How many things which appeared impossible, have been done by resolute men, whose only other resource was to the death!

JM

Maxim LXVIII

There is no security for any sovereign, for any nation, or for any general, if officers are permitted to capitulate in the open field, and to lay down their arms in virtue of conditions, favourable to the contracting party, but contrary to the interest of the army at large. To withdraw from danger, and thereby to involve their comrades in greater peril, is the height of cowardice. Such conduct should be proscribed, declared infamous, and made punishable with death. All generals, officers, and soldiers who capitulate in battle to save their own lives, should be decimated. He who gives the order and those who obey are alike traitors, and deserve capital punishment.

GD

Maxim LXIX

There is but one honourable mode of becoming prisoner of war. That is, by being taken separately; by which is meant, being cut off entirely, and when we can no longer make use of our arms. In this case there can be no conditions, for honour can impose none. We yield to an irresistible necessity.

GD

Maxim LXX

The conduct of a general in a conquered country is full of difficulties. If severe, he irritates and increases the number of his enemies. If lenient, he gives birth to expectations which only render the abuses and vexations inseparable from war the more tolerable. A victorious General must know how to employ severity, justice, and mildness by turn, if he would allay sedition, or prevent it.

GD

Maxim LXXI

Nothing can excuse a general taking advantage of knowledge gained in the service of his country, to fight against it, and to deliver its ramparts to foreign nations; this crime is condemned by the principles of religion, morality, and honour.

JM

Maxim LXXII

A General-in-chief has no right to shelter his mistakes in war under cover of his sovereign, or of a minister, when they are both distant from the scene of operations, and must consequently be either ill informed or wholly ignorant of the actual state of things. Hence it follows that every General is culpable who undertakes the execution of a plan which he considers faulty. It is his duty to represent his reasons, to insist upon a change of plan; in short to give in his resignation rather than to allow himself to become the instrument of his army's ruin. Every General-in-chief who fights a battle in consequence of superior orders, with the certainty of losing it, is equally blameable. In this last-mentioned case, the General ought to refuse obedience; because blind obedience is due only to a military command given by a superior present on the spot at the moment of action. Being in possession of the real state of things, the superior has it then in his power to afford the necessary explanations to the person who executes his order. But supposing a General-in-chief to receive a positive order from his sovereign, directing him to fight a battle, with the further injunction, to yield to his adversary and allow himself to be defeated – ought he obey it? No; if the General should be able to comprehend the meaning or utility of such an order, he should execute it, otherwise he should refuse to obey it.

GD

Maxim LXXIII

The first qualification in a General-in-chief is a cool head – that is, a head which receives just impressions, and estimates things and objects at their real value. He must not allow himself to be elated by good news, or depressed by bad. The impressions he receives, either successively or simultaneously in the course of the day, should be so classed as to take up only the exact place in his mind which they deserve to occupy; since it is upon a just comparison and consideration of the weight due to different impressions that the power of reasoning and of right judgement depends. Some men are so physically and morally constituted as to see everything through a highly coloured medium. They raise up a picture in the mind on every slight occasion, and give to every trivial occurrence a dramatic interest. But whatever knowledge, or talent, or courage, or other good qualities such men may possess, nature has not formed them for the command of armies, or the direction of great military operations.

GD

Maxim LXXIV

To know the country thoroughly; to be able to conduct reconnaissance with skill; to superintend the transmission of orders promptly; to lay down the most complicated movements intelligibly, but in a few words and with simplicity; these are the leading qualifications which should distinguish an officer selected for the head of staff.

GD

Maxim LXXV

It is the duty of the general of artillery to know of all the operations of the army, since he has to furnish arms and ammunition to the different divisions composing it. His intercourse with the commanders of artillery at the outposts should keep him acquainted with all the movements of the army; and the action of his main artillery park should depend on the information thus gained

JM

Maxim LXXVI

To reconnoitre accurately defiles and fords of every description. To provide guides that may be depended upon. To interrogate the curé and postmaster. To establish rapidly a good understanding with the inhabitants. To send out spies. To intercept public and private letters. To translate and analyse their contents. In a word, to be able to answer every question of the general-in-chief when he arrives at the head of the army; these are the qualities which distinguish a good General of advanced posts.

GD

Maxim LXXVII

Generals-in-chief are guided by their own experience or genius. Tactics, evolutions, the science of an artillery or engineering officer may be picked up from books, but the knowledge of the great operations of war can only be acquired by experience, and by the applied study of the campaigns of all the great captains. Gustavus, Turenne and Frederick, as well as Alexander, Hannibal and Caesar have all acted on the same principles. To keep one's forces together, to bear speedily on any point, to b nowhere vulnerable, such are the principles that assure victory; to inspire fear by the reputation of one's arms, that is what maintains the fidelity of allies, and the obedience of conquered nations.

JM

Maxim LXXVIII

Read and re-read the Campaigns of Alexander, Hannibal, Caesar, Gustavus Adolphus, Turenne, Eugene and Frederick; take them for your model, that is the only way of becoming a great captain, to obtain the secrets of the art of war.

JM

Maxim LXXIX

The first principle of a commander-in-chief is to observe clearly what he does, to see if he has all the means of surmounting any obstacle the enemy may place in his way, and if he has made up his mind to do all to overcome those obstacles.

JM

Maxim LXXX

The art of a general, commanding in the van or in the rear, is, without imperilling himself, to keep the enemy back, to delay him, to make him employ three or four hours in marching a league. Tactics alone can give the means of attaining these ends; it is more necessary to cavalry than to infantry, in the van or rear, than in any other position.

JM

Maxim LXXXI

It is rare, and difficult, to possess at one time all the qualities of a great general. What is most desirable (because that draws a man out at once of the common line) is to maintain an equilibrium between his mind and abilities, and his will and courage. If courage prevails more in his composition, the general will undertake designs, the whole possibility of the attainment of which he has not thought out; on the other hand he will not dare to carry his ideas into execution, if his will or courage is inferior to his abilities.

JM

Maxim LXXXII

With a great general, no great action is executed, which is the fruit of chance, or fortune; they are all the result of combination and talent.

JM

Maxim LXXXIII

A commander-in-chief never gives rest either to the victor or to the conquered.

JM

Maxim LXXXIV

An irresolute general who acts without principles or plan, although at the head of an army superior in number to that of the foe, often proves inferior in the battle field. Shuffling, half-measures, lose everything in war.

JM

Maxim LXXXV

To a talented general who has to think out, propose, and execute everything by himself, good judgment and a solid mind are necessary.

JM

Maxim LXXXVI

A cavalry general should possess practical knowledge, know the preciousness of a second even of time, despise life and not trust to chance.

JM

Maxim LXXXVII

A general in the hands of the foe has no power to give orders; to obey them is criminal.

JM

Maxim LXXXVIII

Cavalry of the line should be posted in van, rear, wings, and reserve to support the light cavalry.

JM

Maxim LXXXIX

To wish to keep cavalry for the end of the fight, betrays no idea of the effective power of the charges combined of cavalry and infantry either for attack or defence.

JM

Maxim XC

The strength of cavalry lies in its impetus; but speed alone does not insure victory: what does, is order, harmony, and the proper employment of the reserves.

JM

Maxim XCI

The cavalry should bear a proportion to the infantry of one-fourth in Flanders or Germany; one-twentieth on the Pyrenees or Alps; one-sixth in Italy or Spain.

JM

Maxim XCII

In battle, as in a siege, art is shown in directing fire from many quarters on one point; when the fight is once begun, a leader skil-ful enough to bring to bear on one such point, unknown to the foe, an expected mass of artillery, is sure to carry the day.

JM

Maxim XCIII

The better the infantry, the greater the need to husband it, and support it by good batteries. Good infantry is without doubt the backbone of an army, but if it has had to fight for some length of time against very superior artillery, it will be demoralized and de-stroyed. It may be that a general, a more skilful manoeuvrer than his opponent, may, with his superior infantry, be successful in a part of the campaign, although his artillery is much inferior; but, at the crisis of a general engagement he will bitterly feel his weak-ness in artillery.

JM

Maxim XCIV

A good army of 35,000 to 40,000 men, should in a few days, es-pecially when flanked by a great town or river, render its position unattackable by an army twice its number.

JM

Maxim XCV

War is made up of accidents, and although bound to follow general principles, a general ought not to lose from sight anything which may enable him to profit from these accidents; it is a characteristic of talent. In war there is but one favourable moment: the great thing is to seize it.
JM

Maxim XCVI

A general who keeps fresh troops for the day after the battle almost always is beaten; one must employ, if useful, one's very last man, because, on the day after a complete success, there is no obstacle left; public opinion alone is enough indeed to secure fresh triumphs to the victor
JM

Maxim XCVII

The rules of war demand that a division of an army should avoid fighting alone a whole army which has already scored success.
JM

Maxim XCVIII

When a general has forestalled the investment of a place, has gained a few days on his opponent, he should profit thereby to surround himself by lines of circumvallation; from that moment he has bettered his position, and has acquired, in the general condition of affairs, a new degree of strength, a new element of force.
JM

Maxim XCIX

In war a commandant of a place is not a judge of events; he should hold till the last moment; he deserves death when he surrenders an instant sooner than he is obliged.
JM

Maxim C

Capitulations of bodies, who are cut off during a battle, or on active campaign, are contracts, of which the advantage comes to the contracting parties, but the onerous conditions fall on the prince and the other soldiers. To get out of danger oneself, to make the general's position more dangerous, is clear cowardice.
JM

Maxim CI

Defensive war does not exclude attack, just as offensive war does not exclude defence, although its aim is to force the frontier and invade the enemy's country.

   JM

Maxim CII

The art of war points out that it is necessary to turn and outflank a wing without separating the army.

   JM

Maxim CIII

Field fortifications are always of use, never hurtful, when they are well understood.

   JM

Maxim CIV

An army can pass always and in every season wherever there is room for two men's feel.

   JM

Maxim CV

The conditions of the position occupied should not alone decide the order of battle, which should be determined by the whole circumstances.

   JM

Maxim CVI

Flank marches are to be avoided, and when made should be as short and in as brief a time as possible.

   JM

Maxim CVII

Nothing is more calculated to disorganise and ruin an army altogether than plundering.

   JM

Maxim CVIII

An enemy's praise is suspicious; it is only flattery to a man of honour when given after the cessation of war.

   JM

Maxim CIX

Prisoners of war belong no more to the power for which they have fought; they are all under the safeguard and protection of the honour and generosity of the nation which has disarmed them.
JM

Maxim CX

Conquered provinces should be kept in obedience to their conquerors by moral means, such as making the parishes responsible and establishing a sound administration. Hostages are one of the most powerful of these means, but then they should be numerous and chosen from the chief men ; and inhabitants should understand that the death of the hostages would be the immediate consequence of the violation of faith.
JM

Maxim CXI

The physical configuration of the country; whether living on the mountains or in the plains; the education or discipline of the inhabitants, have more effect than climate on the character of lJ1e troops.
JM

Maxim CXII

All the great captains have done their great deeds by conforming to the rules and natural principles of their art, and by the soundness of their plans, and the proportioned connection maintained between their means and the results they expect, between their efforts and the obstacle to be overcome. They have only succeeded by conforming to rules, whatever might have been the boldness of their designs and the extent of their success. It is on this ground alone that they are our models, and it is only by imitating them that we can hope to rival them.
JM

Maxim CXIII

The first law of maritime tactics should be that, as soon as the admiral has given the signal, each captain should be prepared to make the necessary evolutions for attack of an enemy's ship, to take part in the fight, and support his neighbours.
JM

Maxim CXIV

War on land destroys, in general, more men than war at sea; it is more perilous. the sailor in a squadron fights but once in a campaign; the soldier fights always. The sailor, whatever maybe the dangers and hardships of his element, has less to endure than the soldier. He has with him always his abode, kitchen, hospital, dispensary. The naval armies in the services of France and England, where discipline maintains cleanliness, and to whom experience has taught all the necessary measures for the preservation of health, have fewer men on the sick list than land armies. Independently of danger of fighting, the sailor has that of the sea; but art has so much diminished this latter that it cannot be compared to the perils of the land, popular risings, individual murder, being cut off, surprises by the enemy's light troops, &c.
JM

Maxim CXV

A general, commanding-in-chief a naval army, and a chief of a land army are men who need different qualities. The qualities for the latter are inborn, but those for the former are acquired by experience alone. The art of land warfare is an art of genius, and inspirations. In maritime war nothing depends on genius and inspiration, all is positive, a matter of experience. The sea-general has but need of one science -- navigation. the land-commander has need of all, or of equivalent to all, e.g., that of profiting by universal experience and knowledge. The one has nothing to guess, he knows the position and strength of his antagonists. The other knows nothing for certain, never sees his foe, does not know exactly where he is. When the armies are face to face, the least accident of the ground, the smallest wood, will hide a part of the army. The most practised eye cannot tell if he sees the whole of the hostile army, or but three-quarters. It is by the eyes of the mind, the conjoint use of his reasoning powers, that he sees, knows, and judges. The naval commander has no need of a practised eye, none of the enemy's forces are hidden from him. That which makes the work of the land commander so difficult is the necessity of feeding so many men and animals; if he will not submit to being guided by the commissaries, he will not be able to stir an inch, and his designs will fail. He of the sea is never so embarrassed; he carries everything with him. He has not to reconnoitre, no ground to examine, no battlefield to it; study. The Indian Ocean, and the American Ocean, the Channel, all are but same liquid. The most skilled have no advantage over the least, except by the knowledge of the winds prevailing in such and such a quarter, by '" foreseeing those which ought to prevail, or by atmospheric signs; qualifications acquired by experience, and by experience alone. The land commandant never knows the battle field where he is to operate. His glance is an experienced one, he has no positive information, the data given to him to arrive at a knowledge of localities are so casual that almost nothing is taught by experience. It is the faculty of seizing at once the connection which the ground bears to the nature of countries, it is a gift termed "the soldier's eye" which great generals have received from Nature; yet the observations made on topographical charts, the ease given by education and habit of reading from them, may be of some assistance. A naval commander depends more on his captains than a land commander on his generals. This latter is in a position to take on himself the direct command of the troops to bear on all points, and of remedying false moves. A naval general, personally, has influence but over the men of his own ship. The smoke prevents the signals from being seen, the winds change or are not the same overall space covered by his line. It is then, of all professions, the one in which subalterns may take the most on themselves.

JM

www.ingramcontent.com/pod-product-compliance
Lightning Source LLC
Chambersburg PA
CBHW040853210326
41597CB00029B/4833